WOMEN IN BUSINESS

WOMEN IN BUSINESS

Navigating Career Success

Viki Holton
Research Fellow, Ashridge Business School, UK

and

Fiona Elsa Dent
Director of Executive Education,
Ashridge Business School, UK

First published 2012 by
PALGRAVE MACMILLAN

Palgrave Macmillan in the UK is an imprint of Macmillan Publishers Limited,
registered in England, company number 785998, of Houndmills, Basingstoke,
Hampshire RG21 6XS.

Palgrave Macmillan in the US is a division of St Martin's Press LLC,
175 Fifth Avenue, New York, NY 10010.

Palgrave Macmillan is the global academic imprint of the above companies
and has companies and representatives throughout the world.

Palgrave® and Macmillan® are registered trademarks in the United States,
the United Kingdom, Europe and other countries.

ISBN: 978–0–230–28280–3

This book is printed on paper suitable for recycling and made from fully
managed and sustained forest sources. Logging, pulping and manufacturing
processes are expected to conform to the environmental regulations of the
country of origin.

A catalogue record for this book is available from the British Library.

A catalog record for this book is available from the Library of Congress.

10 9 8 7 6 5 4 3 2 1
21 20 19 18 17 16 15 14 13 12

Printed and bound in Great Britain by
CPI Antony Rowe, Chippenham and Eastbourne

CONTENTS

ACKNOWLEDGMENTS

We would like to thank all the women leaders who took part in the interviews for our research, including:

- Abu Dhabi National Oil Company – Aseel Hamoodi, Vice-President of Business Support
- Buckinghamshire County Council – Gillian Hibberd, Strategic Director of Resources and Business Transformation
- Cambridge Display Technology – Ilaria Grizzi, Vice-President, Technology Development
- China Post – Yao Hong, Vice-President
- Cisco Systems Europe – Wendy Mars, Director, Data Centre and Virtualization
- Danfoss – Birgitte Ladefoged, HR Senior Director
- Ernst & Young – Caroline Artis, Senior Tax Partner
- Google UK – Sarah Speake, Strategic Marketing Director
- International Hotels Group – Rajni Gupta, Director of Compliance and Corporate Governance
- Japan Tobacco International – Marie-Hélène Dubé, Media Relations Director
- Johnson & Johnson Medical Devices – Rosemary Grant, UK Country Manager (until January 2011)
- Merck – Hester van Blaauw, Global Purchasing Manager
- Mott MacDonald Singapore – Shirley Sivakumaran, Senior Project Manager
- National Trust – Beccy Speight, Director, Midlands Region
- NHS – Gill Collinson, Director of Engagement
- NHS – Professor Dame Sally Davies, Chief Medical Officer and Chief Scientific Adviser, Department of Health and the National Health Service, and Governor at Ashridge Business School

- Red Door Communications – Catherine Warne, Chief Executive
- Shell – Tanya Kabalin, Global Supply Manager UK and Nordic Regions
- Sinopec Corporation – Guimei Pan, Senior Vice-President

We are grateful to everyone who took the time to complete our survey questionnaire – and to our colleagues in Ashridge and others who helped us develop our ideas during this project. Special thanks to Jan Rabbetts for her encouragement, patience and attention to detail as our in-house editor – we couldn't have done it without you. Also, many thanks to Ali Abington, Eileen Mullins, Judy Curd, Michelle Moore, Barbara Wang, Helen Lockett and Shihong Mu for their help.

1

OVERVIEW

Based on our experience of working with many women in our role as consultant, trainer, coach and researcher, we continue to hear about women who have to deal with significant challenge and inequality in their career and we felt that researching this area to determine and report on the current landscape for women would be a useful contribution for industry and organizations. This book is aimed at,

- individual women who would like to check out where they are with their career, and how they might improve their career opportunities;
- managers and colleagues who work with female colleagues;
- anyone interested in business and diversity.

This book is also written for organizations to help them review how women are treated and to ask some fundamental questions, for instance, whether there is a level playing field for men and women. We hope that our book and our research findings will challenge organizations, HR directors and chief executives to answer the following questions:

- Can you put your hand on your heart and say that there are equal opportunities for women in your organization?
- When did you last ask women this question?
- Are women equally likely to be managers at every level of your organization?
- Are there stereotypes about women and about their leadership style?
- How can you improve equality and demonstrate how this connects to the bottom line and creates a more productive, effective business?

The research data for this book included a self-completion survey completed by over 1,400 women, 39 percent of whom are senior managers, and a further 30 percent are directors or chief executives. It is a large survey and we believe it's probably one of the biggest European studies undertaken in recent years. We also interviewed 20 women leaders to help us appreciate their career issues, what had helped or hindered their progress and also to hear their stories of what it means to be a woman manager in the 21st century.

There has been a good deal of literature – both in the academic press and, more recently, in the business press – about diversity, but much of this focuses on issues that individual women face. Few projects look at the current situation for women leaders and consider the practical implications of this for employers as well as for individuals. Our research aims to address this gap in the literature and builds on our own knowledge and experience of working with women who attend Ashridge Business School programs. There are around 1,200 women manager delegates each year (30 percent of the total number), usually sponsored by their companies and they represent a diverse group from a range of disciplines who may be working in the UK, elsewhere in Europe or internationally.

The program of our research involved two distinct phases. First we designed a large-scale survey questionnaire which was distributed to women managers nationally in the UK and internationally who were operating in public and private sector organizations. The questionnaire focused on career issues and examined:

- issues that have blocked, or helped, career progress;
- leadership style;
- opinions about whether men and women are treated equally in organizations.

We designed our research to focus on women's experiences – rather than a methodology which compared men and women. A second phase of the research comprised a number of in-depth interviews with senior women leaders; a few are entrepreneurs who have built their own successful businesses as well as a range of achievers from the public and private sector. In the public and not-for-profit sector these included women working in the National Trust, the National Health Service and at Buckinghamshire County Council. Organizations represented included Abu Dhabi National Oil Company, Cambridge Display Technology, Cisco, China Post, Danfoss, Ernst & Young, Google, International Hotels Group (IHG), Japan Tobacco International (JTI), Johnson & Johnson Medical Devices, Merck, Mott MacDonald,

Red Door Communications, Shell and Sinopec. Most of the individuals are named in the acknowledgements section at the beginning of this book though some preferred to remain anonymous. The total group includes a mix of nationalities such as Danish, Chinese, French/Canadian, Sri Lankan, South African/British, British and Dutch. They represent a variety of disciplines – including IT, finance, strategy, marketing and operational roles – as well as ages ranging from mid-30s to late 50s. Their achievements are impressive and a number are at the most senior executive level, such as being a member of a main board in a multinational, or a country manager with significant budget and operational responsibilities.

The interviews focused on how these women leaders have achieved their career success and what knowledge, leadership style and expertise has helped them. We asked them to tell us about critical incidents in their career. Some of these examples are negative and had been hard to deal with at the time but the majority are positive. A particular theme is the amount of encouragement and coaching they received from managers, mentors and individuals who could see their abilities and potential and helped them along the way. Another is their self confidence and belief and determination to succeed.

HOW TO USE THIS BOOK

The book deals with the key issues for women managers (see Chapters 3 to 10), as well as a bit of the history, which can be found in Chapter 2. Appendix A highlights women's achievements from 1903 through to 2011, so if you are interested to know who some of the pioneers were, this is the place to look! It is not confined to business success and also covers some political and legal events. Some of the early names included may be unfamiliar but others will be better known – Christine Lagarde for example, appointed head of the International Monetary Fund in 2011, is the first woman to be appointed to that role. The same is true for Indra Nooyi who in 2006 became the first woman chief executive at Pepsico.

Who should read this book? We have tried to write a practical book that will help individual women with their careers. However, it also offers many ideas and tips that will enable businesses to create a better environment for women. There are various places you can dip into the book and the chapter headings are noted below. For example if you want to look at women's leadership style then take a look at Chapter 6, but if you are more interested to read first about career promoters or barriers these can be found in Chapters 4 and 5 respectively. In Appendix B there is a copy of the survey results – though this does not include any of the qualitative comments.

The book also offers some information (about the current organizational landscape) and advice in Chapter 7, which is written specifically for organizations. Each chapter has advice, key points or summary illustrations that we hope will make for easy reading. And if you have time and prefer a traditional approach you can of course start at the first page and read through each chapter in turn.

CHAPTER CONTENTS

1. Overview – an introduction and description of the research approach	**2. The Historical Perspective** – some key events and issues that have happened for women in business
3. Early Career Issues – summarizes the events which are important during women's early career stages	**4. Career Promoters** – reviews more generally what helps women in their career and distinguishes critical events and experiences
5. Career Barriers – what is it that holds women back and stops them achieving their full potential?	**6. Women in Leadership** – identifies a variety of different leadership styles and considers the impact of each of these
7. The Organizational Landscape – describes what life is like in the 21st century for many women in business	**8. Advice and What I Wish I'd Known Earlier In My Career** – advice for organizations and for individual women
9. Strategies for Career Success – includes a framework and ideas for helping women develop their careers	**10. Final Thoughts** – about women managers and what might happen in future
Appendix A: A Timeline of Women's Achievements, 1903–2011	Appendix B: Questionnaire Quantitative Analysis

WHAT THIS BOOK IS AND WHAT IT IS NOT

The aim of this book is to report on our research about the career success and some of the continuing challenges for women leaders. It does not describe every detail about organizational life in terms of HR policies or career development structures. Nor do we cover in detail the experience of what is likely to happen in smaller firms – though women who worked in smaller firms reported similar experiences to those in large companies. The majority of the women who took part in the survey are working in companies with 1,000 or more staff. Similarly, most of the women leaders we interviewed work in the corporate world (or in large public sector organizations).

2

THE HISTORICAL PERSPECTIVE

This is a great time for women managers and it feels in my organization as if we're pushing against an open door – the company is keen to create a better environment for the women who work here.

Interview quote

Regardless of which country or profession you look at, the progress of women managers has been pretty slow. Whether you consider the public or the private sector, different countries, different industry sectors or the situation at junior, middle or senior management level, change is happening, but at a slow pace. Our own experience of working in a leading business school means that we talk to many women managers. Some are already at middle and senior executive levels and others are just starting their career. It's great to know that some of these women work for organizations with a total commitment to diversity and equality issues, as the quotes from our survey illustrate:

People here are judged on merit not on gender.

I can honestly say that this is a truly diverse company and within this sector of the business – Consumer Lifestyle – I do not think of women versus men when making judgements – it is about what they deliver and their future potential to go further in this organisation.

Some organizations these days include a section about diversity and opportunities for women on their website. The healthcare giant Johnson & Johnson illustrates this on its website listing each year through 'diversity awards and recognition'; see www.jnj.com/connect/about-jnj/diversity/awards/ Google also does this, www.google.com/diversity.

However, it is evident that not all organizations are as good with regard to diversity. Although there has been change over the past few years – not least a growing number of women at senior management level – we also hear about issues which remain a barrier for women, issues which are depressingly similar to what was said by earlier generations. A few of these points are illustrated below with quotes from our survey and the interviews conducted for this research:

Some men don't like working with women.

The decisions here made by women managers are checked by someone else; that doesn't happen for the men!

I was told I was 'confrontational', but I don't think that this label would have been used to a man for the same type of behaviour which I would describe differently – as challenging and not confrontational.

There are those women whom we mentioned earlier who are working in organizations that are gender-neutral. However, the majority view is with those – nearly one in two respondents – who say it's harder for women to succeed in their organizations. It's a finding which indicates that there is much more that could be done to create a better, fairer, working environment for women managers.

WHY EQUALITY MATTERS

The rest of this chapter provides an overview of what has happened for women managers but before that we should perhaps explain why we think the topic of equality and diversity is important. Does it matter whether women are equally likely as their male colleagues to be a chief executive, a member of the board, a head of operations or a country manager? We do think it is important – for business reasons as well as for the equality and ethical dimensions.

Some key reasons are briefly described below. Some businesses understand how diversity links to the bottom line such as the buying power link which exists between women customers (the external environment) and women in decision-making roles (the internal environment) of the organization, an argument which is also true for disability, sexual diversity and race and religious differences. Minority groups for instance may also represent a significant market share.

Edward Hubbard's book *The Diversity Scorecard: Evaluating the Impact of Diversity on Organisational Performance*[1] has more information about the business case and how to measure diversity.

A second issue is the added value that often emerges from creating diverse teams – as opposed to a 'group think' across a business. Demographics are another factor. The increasing number of well-educated women in many countries is closely linked to society's expectation that this should also be reflected in a growing number of women in management. This is something which is happening currently in some Middle Eastern countries, evident in events such as the third annual Women in Leadership Forum Middle East held in Abu Dhabi in November 2011. http://website.naseba.com/wilforum. Ashridge has also contributed to the women's program for the Mohammed bin Rashid Al Maktoum Foundation in Dubai.

Another reason – and something that business has been surprisingly slow to understand – is around talent management. Gender equality and diversity is about attracting and promoting the most talented staff, a point noted by one of the most admired chief executives in the UK back in the mid-1990s:

> *Any major company which does not attempt to attract women specialists and managers denies itself full access to the very best abilities available. Equal opportunity is not about looking good and feeling good – it is sound business sense...*
>
> Sir Colin Marshall (now Lord Marshall of Knightsbridge) when Chairman of British Airways, with permission

This view is highlighted in a *Harvard Business Review* article over a decade ago by Doug McCracken, 'Winning the Talent War for Women'. It was written when he was chief executive at the accounting firm Deloitte and describes the changes (and even talks about it as a revolution) required in order to create a better environment for women.[2]

There are also increasingly legal and financial penalties if employers get it wrong – as highlighted by the cases below. Most awards are far less costly but these illustrate just how high the price of discrimination can be.

In June 2011 Donna Kassman, a senior manager in a New York professional services firm, filed a gender discrimination class action case for $350 million (£213 million).[3]

In 2011 Maureen Murphy and Anna Francis claimed sex discrimination for £1.5 million from a Japanese bank based in the City of London.[4]

In 2008 in the UK Gill Switalski won a case against a financial services firm – the settlement was £19 million.[5]

A few years earlier in 2004 a US bank settled a case in the US before the trial for sex discrimination for $54 million.[6] The largest sex discrimination case in North America is a class action against a major retailer and this is still (May 2011) progressing through the court system. Betty Dukes worked in the Pittsburg store and was one of a small group to bring a case against the retailer back in 2001 but the courts have decided that 1.5 million women staff (and ex-employees) cannot bring a unified case against the company but can pursue individual claims.[7]

The rest of this chapter describes some of the key developments for women beginning with the 1900s; then we take a look at the last years of the 20th century and finally what's happened more recently. There is also a timeline shown in Appendix A which highlights women's achievements over the years.

EARLY YEARS OF CHANGE

One of the key changes for women was gaining the right to vote, which happened at different times across the world. New Zealand gave women the right to vote before 1900 but in Europe it happened a few years later, and the first country to do this was Finland. It seems such a long time ago and it's fascinating to see how change happened differently. For instance, women in Russia – partly because of communism – got the vote long before this happened in Spain, France or Italy. Switzerland and Portugal were later still – women didn't get the right to vote there until the 1970s.

It's worth pointing out that it is still a contentious issue in parts of the Middle East. Some countries are missing from the list that follows – Saudi Arabia for example held local elections in 2005 where men could vote for the first time but not women. In 2015 women will be allowed to vote. And whilst women are increasingly involved in business in Saudi this remains the only country (as of spring 2012) where women are not allowed to drive a car.

When women got the vote – a selective list of dates

1869	Wyoming Territory in the US is the first place in the world to give votes to women
1881	Women who are property owners in the Isle of Man are eligible to vote (universal rights are given in 1919)
1893	New Zealand gives women the vote
1902	Australia gives women the right to vote, although Aboriginal women are not eligible until 1967 when, along with Aboriginal men, they are granted full citizenship
1906	Finland is the first country in Europe to give women the vote
1913	Norway
1915	Denmark and Iceland
1917	Russia
1918	United Kingdom (partial), Germany, Canada, Austria
1919	Netherlands, Belgium
1920	The US, but not Native American women
1925	Italy (in local elections)
1928	United Kingdom (all women were eligible to vote the following year in the 1929 General Election), Ireland
1930	South Africa, but only to white women. Indian and 'colored' women won the vote in 1984 and black women in 1994
1931	Spain
1934	Brazil
1944	France, Japan
1945	Italy
1946	Kenya, Palestine
1947	Pakistan
1948	Israel, Iraq
1949	China
1950	India
1952	Greece
1953	Mexico
1956	Egypt, Tunisia, Mauritius
1957	Malaysia
1962	Algeria, Monaco
1971	Switzerland
1974	Jordan
1976	Portugal
1984	Lichtenstein
1999	Qatar
2001	Bahrain

(Continued)

2005	Kuwait
2006	United Arab Emirates (limited rights to vote for a certain number of seats on the National Council)

Main source: With permission. BBC Radio 4 Website, 'Woman's Hour' Timeline. Accessed October 2010, www.bbc.co.uk/radio4/womanshour/timeline/votes_to_women.shtml

Checked against list at International Women's Democracy Center published on http://www.iwdc.org/resources/suffrage.htm, accessed January 2010.

In the early part of the 20th century there were some outstanding women including those who lobbied for the right to be journalists, war correspondents and to report the news – something that was resisted at the time by many. It's almost forgotten now and it's something that we take for granted today but it was a tough fight for those pioneer women.

Alix Meynell was also a pioneer as one of the first women graduates to join the UK Civil Service back in 1925. Until then women were not permitted to sit the entry administrative examinations. Alix Meynell[8] had great abilities as a thinker and administrator and during a stellar career was admired by her colleagues and by the politicians she worked for. She retired in the mid-1950s as one of the most senior civil servants and so it might have been expected that a younger generation of talented women would simply follow in her footsteps. However, it was only during the 1970s that the number of women in local and national government began to increase significantly. Currently there are 21 percent women leading around 360 local authorities in the UK.[9] At the senior level of the Civil Service there is a group of talented women but it still remains a fairly small, select group. A marker of the slow general progress is evident in the data displayed in the following table – in early 2012 there were only two women mayors in 20 major cities (taken at random) across a range of countries.

But let us return to the 1970s when many large employers in the private sector began to actively recruit and provide opportunities for women graduates as managers. Until that point there had been limited opportunities. A number of professions and organizations had a policy for women to retire upon marriage. Ed Brandt,[10] the company historian for Dow Chemicals, noted that not until 1980 did a woman (other than Grace Dow, a family member) join the Board of Directors. It was typical of the situation in many other businesses and today – in every country around the world, from North America, across Europe and through to Japan and China – it remains unusual to find

Number of women mayors – in 20 large cities

City	Country	City population	Mayor
Tokyo	Japan	8,653,000	Shintaro Ishihara
New York	US	8,364,000	Michael Bloomberg
London	UK	7,557,000	Boris Johnson
Hong Kong	China	7,055,000	Donald Tsang
Sydney	Australia	4,400,000	**Clover Moore**
Los Angeles	US	3,834,000	Antonio Villaraigosa
Berlin	Germany	3,432,000	Klaus Wowereit
Madrid	Spain	3,213,000	Alberto Ruiz-Gallardón
Chicago	US	2,853,000	Rahm Emanuel
Rome	Italy	2,732,000	Gianni Alemanno
Toronto	Canada	2,571,000	Rob Ford
Paris	France	2,113,000	Bertrand Delanoë
Vienna	Austria	1,681,000	Michael Häupl
Milan	Italy	1,302,000	**Letizia Moratti**
Copenhagen	Denmark	1,096,000	Frank Jensen
Brussels	Belgium	958,000	Freddy Thielemans
Stockholm	Sweden	826,000	Sten Nordin
Amsterdam	Netherlands	762,000	Eberhard van der Laan
Oslo	Norway	584,000	Fabian Stang
Helsinki	Finland	583,000	Jussi Pajunen

Note: Entries in bold indicate women. Cities selected from City Mayors website (www.citymayors. com/statistics/largest-cities-mayors-1.html), accessed January 2012. With permission to publish.

women in the boardroom. Ashridge surveyed the UK trends during the 1990s and we found that most of the women who were appointed were invited to join as non-executive directors.[11] These are external appointments and by comparison we found few women promoted from within companies to take the more important executive board appointments.

AT THE END OF THE 20TH CENTURY

By the end of the 1980s a group of people were so concerned about the situation for women managers in Europe that they decided to set up a support network to help individuals and to encourage and lobby business to be more progressive. Those involved felt that Europe was in danger of being left behind by the advances that seemed to be happening in North America. The group was the European Women's Management Development Network (EWMD) and at the beginning they believed that ten years would be sufficient to achieve their aims.

A review at the end of this first decade concluded that, yes, some encouraging and significant changes had happened. Not least of these was the 'Taten statt worte' or 'Deeds not Words' campaign in Switzerland, which was created by Elisabeth Michel-Alder. She was a charismatic woman and attracted sponsorship from a number of leading businesses. However, it was evident that equality was still very much 'work in progress'; and so the need for EWMD was as strong as when it first started. Now we are in the 21st century; EWMD continues to work with organizations and to provide support, practical help and role models for many hundreds of women managers. www.ewmd.org

Another significant change in the UK at the end of the 1990s was the decision by Business in the Community (a charity led by the Prince of Wales) to launch 'Opportunity 2000'. It was a radical approach as employers who joined the campaign were expected to set their own targets to improve the situation for women in the workforce – nothing like this had existed before. In fact few organizations dedicated time or resources to diversity issues. Ashridge, under the leadership of Valerie Hammond, provided advice and the research framework to launch the campaign. It was clear that a few enlightened organizations were willing to become trail blazers and their leadership was really impor-tant to create credibility with the rest of the business community. Until that time equality and diversity issues were rarely considered as a mainstream business topic and few people appreciated the link between diversity and talent management.

There was a good deal of discussion before the launch about timing – the UK was in the midst of a recession and so perhaps employers would not be willing to commit to the action required. There was even talk of abandoning target setting (which was as controversial then as it is today); some said that 'no targets' might encourage more organiza-tions to sign up. Others believed that targets were critical for success on the basis of what doesn't get measured in business doesn't happen. It was also assumed – as indicated in the campaign title – that again there would be a finite lifespan, up to the year 2000, after which time the aims would have been achieved.

However, as 2000 came closer it was evident, as with EWMD, that the efforts of Opportunity 2000 were just beginning rather than ending. There were some high points during that decade such as the appointment in 1993 of Penny Hughes as President and Chief Executive at Coca-Cola UK. This was a key appointment and it seemed a breakthrough for someone who was only in her 30s but these events were relatively few and far between. So a new name, 'Opportunity Now', was chosen and the campaign has gone from strength to strength. Annual awards are now part of the process as are individual targets set by each organization. These targets are crucial in bringing about change. In 2012 Opportunity Now will have existed for more than two decades and continues to ensure that women and men are treated equally. The campaign has not yet moved beyond the UK where over 300 organizations are involved representing over 5 million individuals in a workforce of some 29 million. www.opportunitynow.org.uk

From the work of both Opportunity Now and EWMD it is clear that the organizations involved which are most successful in developing women are those that take most action (rather than merely talking) to ensure this happens. The phrase 'greenwash' (as opposed to white-wash) has been used to describe organizations where there is more talk than action about green issues such as sustainability. A similar phenomenon happens in diversity where organizations put a good spin on what they say yet in reality take little action.

Diversity should be treated in the same way as any other type of change program. A strong steer from the chief executive is critical along with a clear action plan and where diversity results are linked to performance and rewards then, not surprisingly, change occurs. There are still a lot of skeptics who argue whether it's possible to link financial rewards to diversity but as the quote below from one of our interviews illustrates, it does work:

> It's possible to have a financial rewards system that recognises when people have a diverse team, whether this is about cultures or gender. It's important as there is then an appreciation of diversity.

In contrast some organizations publish an equality statement and believe that this, together with pronouncements about a general commitment to equality, will make change happen. It rarely does. It's rather like publishing a statement that the organization wishes to expand into a new market. Without an action plan, targets and measures of success, little is likely to change. Although the know-how about how to be successful was described back in the 1990s with the work of the American Roosevelt Thomas[12] and others, diversity remains a tough challenge for many businesses.

AT THE BEGINNING OF THE 21ST CENTURY

In our view, without the Opportunity Now campaign, the UK would have made far less progress. In 2005 the leading German newspaper *Der Spiegel*, ahead of the announcement that Angela Merkel was to be the first female Chancellor, published an article with the headline statement,

Berlin may get a female Chancellor, but it's still a man's world.[13]

A similar comment might also be heard in Japan, where only 8 percent of managers are women.[14] Tokiko Shimizu, who in 2010 became the Bank of Japan's first female branch chief,[15] said that women are often not given the same responsibilities as their male colleagues – this is crucial as it means women lack key skills which are required for more senior appointments.

The number of women managers across Europe has increased gradually during the 1990s and during the early part of the 21st century – as indicated in the Eurostat data shown later in this section – but many barriers remain. There are still few women at more senior levels of management, and more than one major employer has no women among the senior team (as opposed to board level). An example which illustrates this is a large multinational based in Asia. The company has regularly held a senior leadership event every 18 months or so for the past six years. Over 400 people have attended the meetings so far but there have been only two women. Of course some readers may say, *'well, only two women have attended because there aren't any working in the organisation capable of being among the executive cadre'*. That may be partly true but the reality often is that an overwhelmingly male executive group which has existed for many years finds it hard to change and accommodate women. It is easier, simpler and more comfortable to continue recruiting in their own image.

Some major Chinese employers for example are known to prefer recruiting male graduates (information from our research interviews),

This point is highlighted by the following extract taken in 2010 from the China web pages of a major international professional services company, which feels the need to state that it is different and willing to consider recruiting both men and women:

> Gender is definitely not a selection criteria and we pride ourselves on being an equal opportunity employer. *Accessed October 2010*

Sexism exists elsewhere, including some parts of the Square Mile – the City of London's financial area –[16] and in the US on Wall Street.[17] Dominique Senequier explained in a *Financial Times* interview[18] that being a woman in private equity attracts a lot of jealousy from men. (She is one of a few senior women in private equity investment in France.) One woman we interviewed also highlights traditional attitudes towards women which prevail in parts of the Middle East:

> *I frequently travel in the Middle East and work with colleagues in Qatar and Dubai but there is a different attitude elsewhere and I would not go to some other countries where women are less welcome – it is simpler to send a male colleague instead.*
>
> **Interview quote**

Susan Sabanci Dincer, chairman of Akbank, one of the largest Turkish banks, was asked about sexism. She said that Turkey is notoriously sexist but this is not the case in the finance sector and that in her bank there are many women managers.[19]

It's often assumed that women managers do better in the US[20] but a review of what is happening at senior levels reveals the same trends that are evident elsewhere. There are still remarkably few women at chief executive and board level – only 15 among the Fortune 500 chief executives.[21] Irene Rosenfeld at Kraft Foods, Carol Bartz at Yahoo! until 2011, Anne Mulcahy and Ursula Burns at Rank Xerox and Carly Fiorina who until 2005 was at Hewlett Packard, are some well-known chief executives. When Anne Mulcahy retired as chief executive in 2009 at Rank Xerox and handed the role over to Ursula Burns this was the first time that one woman succeeded another among Fortune 500 companies. As of early 2012 this remains the only example.

The lack of women is also evident in some organizations which surround business such as Davos, the key world business meeting which is hosted annually by the World Economic Forum in Davos, Switzerland.[22] Among the 81 key business leaders attending the 2009 meeting (from an edited list of delegates published) only four are women. So it's interesting to note that in 2011 the WEF decided to propose a minimum quota, that the 100 key member companies should include one woman (at least) in each team of five senior executives who attend.[23] We should perhaps add here that whilst quotas can be a bad idea – if they simply use gender rather than ability – they can be extremely helpful where, as at Davos, there are plenty of capable women who are not selected for a variety of reasons. Another example of a 'good' quota is a request by companies to executive search or recruitment agencies to ensure women candidates are around a third on any list considered.

There is also some encouraging news of women's progress with the increasing numbers of women graduates and the trends for management generally. The Eurostat data show the change from 2001 to 2007 – nearly a third of managers across the 27 countries in the Eurozone (EU27) are women. Some countries show little change between the two survey dates – for example in France and Spain the number of women managers over this period is virtually unchanged. The data also highlight a universal salary gender gap although the amount varies across the different countries. Data about pay have been collated in the UK since 1974 and in 2011; for the first time since the survey started, women (at junior levels) achieved equality with men.[24] Yet, overall the survey indicates a two-tier workplace as despite this narrowing at the junior levels, the pay gap has actually widened at more senior levels.

Italy appears to have witnessed more change than most where the number of women managers has jumped from 17.8 percent to 33.5 percent. However, other research published in 2010 indicates that a lower figure may more accurately reflect the current situation. Elisa Martinuzzi and Flavia Krause-Jackson[25] report on a survey by Gea-Consulenti Associati of 1,800 companies. This study found only 809 women among the 11,730 managers (including chief executives and chairmen) in all the companies which were surveyed. If we accept these more recent data as representative of Italy then women hold only just over 7 percent of management roles. This would mean that Italy lags a long way behind the progress in Spain, France, Germany and the UK.

Juggling Work and Family: One reason Martinuzzi and Krause-Jackson suggest for such low numbers is the lack of support in Italy

Proportion of female managers in the EU
(selected list of countries) %

———— 2001
•••••• 2007

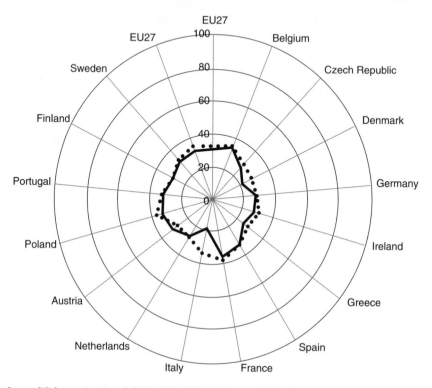

Source: With permission, ref: 2010-COP-411/396444 issued 7 July 2010.

for working mothers, which means women feel they have to choose between a career and family. The tensions created from juggling work and career are common to many countries – working parents and more particularly women who also happen to be working mothers in Germany, China, North America, Holland, France, Switzerland and Asia all describe difficulties that this causes. Sylvia Ann Hewlett[26] talks about women's non-linear careers in the US and the problems created when women who have taken time out to raise a family re-enter the workplace.

How hard, or how easy, this might be is partly due to the attitudes of those around us: *in Germany women are seen as bad mothers if they work, so there are few women managers.*[27] One senior woman director – in

Northern Europe – interviewed in our research said that although she is happy to talk about her young family with her own team, she does not mention them to others in the organization, *as I feel it may affect how I am judged as a manager.* Her concern is that she will be judged more negatively as a working mother. An interview with one of the most senior women in the UK media sector, Jay Hunt, highlights the challenges of struggling with a senior role, long hours and a new baby.[28]

These points are emphasized in McKinsey's 2010 report 'Women Matter'.[29] They surveyed over 400 senior managers to ask about barriers for women. One of the major issues identified by women and men alike is this double burden of work and family, which is compounded by the demanding work model required by many organizations of anywhere/anytime working.

Some businesses are keen to help staff balance work with family commitments. Twenty-five years ago, in 1985, the American *Working Mothers* magazine launched awards for the best companies for working mothers. A few employers – such as Johnson & Johnson and IBM – have the distinction of being on the Top 100 list every year and the Top 10 companies in 2010[30] are shown below. All are outstanding for their family-friendly policies and management attitudes.

Ernst & Young	General Mills	IBM
Bank of America	Deloitte	Discovery Communications
KPMG	WellStar Health System	PriceWaterhouse Coopers
University of Wisconsin Hospital and Clinics		

Note: A similar survey has been run in Canada for over ten years now, see www.canadastop100.com/family/ Accessed May 2011. *Sunday Times* also holds annual awards – The Top 50 Employers for Women.

Employers willing to look at ways to support working parents – because it is both men and women who are impacted by this – can make a significant difference. A key issue is the need to ensure that part-time working is a career option rather than something which is career limiting. In the UK some years ago the idea of 'career breaks' made it far simpler to take time out for children and then return to their employer with either the same or similar work. It represented a win-win situation, the individual returned to a fulfilling career and the organization was able to retain talented staff. In Holland the idea of working a four-day week has become increasingly attractive among professional men,[31] significantly changing their earlier, more rigid work patterns. It's too early to say whether this is a trend that might spread into other countries but changing social attitudes will help create a more progressive attitude towards working parents.

THE SITUATION AT BOARD LEVEL

As mentioned earlier there are fewer women at more senior executive levels. The data given in the table that follows were published by *Der Spiegel*. They also polled 30 top German businesses asking them about their view on quotas – only one replied positively about using these to help increase the number of women managers.[32]

Percentage of women in top management at major stock market-listed companies (2009)

	Percentage
Norway	42
Sweden	27
Germany	13
EU (27 countries)	11
Italy	4

Source: Süddeutsche Zeitung, DIW, European Commission, *Der Spiegel online, with permission*. www.spiegel.de/international/germany/0,1518,683869,00.html, accessed February 2011.

If we glance over the past few years the number of women chief executives is very small. An international survey of 2,000 CEOs between 1995 and 2000 found only 29 women.[33] But the current scenario indicates similar data with few women at the top. One European survey in 2010[34] indicates that on average women are only around 12 percent of board members. In Norway it was high, but in Portugal it was as low as 4 percent! Figures quoted for Brazil[35] are also low – at 8 percent. A Dutch survey[36] in 2010 found that the majority (61 percent) of the 99 leading companies there listed on Euronext, Amsterdam, do not have any women at board level. In the UK the statistics are better but 32 percent of the leading 150 FTSE companies (the largest companies) are without a woman at board level according to a survey by Spencer Stuart.[37] Further somber information is the fact that among the 150 chief executives there are only seven women.

On the other side of the world, a report from New Zealand[38] reveals women hold less than 10 percent of director appointments among the top 100 companies listed on the stock exchange NZX, a figure unchanged since 2008. In Australia it is lower as there are six female chief executives among the top 200 companies.[39] The European survey (mentioned earlier) also looked for the first time at the Chairman of the Board role and found only 48 women among 1,110 boards reviewed. The concern over the low number of women at board level in the UK has recently become a topic for public debate,[40] so much so that the government asked Lord Davies to report on the situation. He suggested a number of practical improvements but stopped short of recommending quotas.

Illustration: The women's quota at Deutsche Telekom

At certain times, a single company (or a small group) can be a trendsetter for others to follow. We've seen this in recent years in terms of sustainability issues. Something similar is happening in Germany where Deutsche Telekom has voluntarily decided to introduce a women's quota for executive positions. (As noted earlier the topic of targets and legal quotas is controversial.)

The introduction of the women's quota at Deutsche Telekom initially created enormous media interest. During the first year of introduction, HR Director Thomas Sattelberger says, the interest from international as well as from national media sources regarding that topic exceeded that of all previous years by far. 'Two thirds of the responses' were positive:

> but we also received extremely negative reactions against our planned interventions into the 'natural flow' of career decisions. Regardless of whether the response from others was positive or not, we could contribute to the initiation of a broad societal debate around chances for women in management. Apart from that, the discussion gathered momentum in the political sphere – a debate in which four federal ministers gave serious considerations to quota regulations and challenged companies to act. In this debate Deutsche Telekom acts as a catalyst within the leading German companies of the DAX30 group. The other DAX companies are currently about to set voluntary commitments as well.

(Continued)

We asked Thomas Sattelberger for his advice for other companies thinking about introducing a quota:

the business cases behind diversity in management give a clear rationale for increasing the proportion of women at the top. Nevertheless, as long as men are among themselves on executive floors, reproducing themselves in so called 'closed systems', actions based on rationality alone will not help to change anything. Closed social systems cannot be opened by means of goodwill alone; it needs a shift in mindset and culture guided and guarded by corporate regulatory policy. Those in power to design and shape social systems are the ones being challenged to prescribe and create a new permeable fabric. This fabric must be supported by KPIs (key performance indicators). At Deutsche Telekom we therefore steer and monitor the entire talent and career pathway in order to ensure fair opportunities in all recruiting and promotion decisions, but also in processes and activities like short-lists for executive appointments, assessment centres and management audits or the participation in executive development programmes.

One key issue identified for women in order to advance their careers at Deutsche Telekom is a family-friendly working culture:

Women need an environment where they don't have to make a choice between family and career. The same applies increasingly for men. We need to enable ambitious employees to take the time necessary for family and private life alongside their careers, encourage female and male managers alike to engage more in family life and opt for temporary or continuous part-time work even in leadership positions. In male-dominated corporate cultures women consciously contemplate if they should take the next step on the career ladder in the face of increasing power struggles and decreasing free time. We need to change this type of corporate culture in order to shape the environment for successful careers of women and men alike. That is to say, we need to replace the face-time (presenteeism) culture by a flexible step-out step-in culture.

The New York Times[41] reported that in 2010 no women led any of the 30 largest German companies at the chief executive level. In each country a Catch-22 situation exists. A key ingredient for board level appointments in blue-chip[42] organizations is experience working for other PLCs (public limited companies). As so few women have this experience it means the group of potential candidates is restricted and one senior woman in the City of London observed this also means men are likely to be selected as they already hold the vast majority of non-executive board appointments in other blue-chip organizations.[43]

However, there are many creative ways to resolve such issues such as mentoring, coaching and job shadowing but only a few large organizations appear to take such action. One example might be enabling staff below board level to follow members of the board and attend various meetings throughout the year thereby providing them with key experience and knowledge that otherwise would be difficult to gain. It would be good to see more organizations looking at different ways to bring high caliber women into their board. Another approach might be a coaching structure to assist women (and men) at lower levels to understand the skills required and take away some of the mystique that is often associated with these most senior roles. A number of Danish employers including Lego, Bang & Olufsen, Danfoss and Carlsberg signed an agreement[44] at the end of 2010 with the government to review how to increase the number of women at board level. In the UK a mentoring program was set up in 2003 to match chairmen from the leading, FTSE 100, companies with potential women directors.[45]

How women gain the skills and knowledge required to step up to these roles is unfortunately often left too much to chance. Mentoring and coaching can help considerably. Taking charge of key projects and major change initiatives helps to improve skills and to demonstrate the qualities essential for a chief executive, for example re-engineering the manufacturing and supply chain for a multinational reducing the operating costs by a third over a five year period.[46] Many organizations find that on close examination there is a gender bias about who gets these key 'stretch' assignments.

An exciting development is the launch of the 30% Club in the UK at the end of 2010. Led by Sir Win Bischoff, Chairman of Lloyds Bank, the ambitious aim is for at least 30 percent female representation at board level within five years (which will be 2015) and the Club is targeted at those key decision makers, the Board Chairmen. It is probably the first such club in any country and may well encourage similar campaigns elsewhere. Two or three key business leaders in any country (or sector) might easily create enough energy and interest for such a campaign to be successful (www.30percentclub.org.uk).

TAKING THE MBA TRACK

With regard to Master of Business Administration (MBA) qualifications the data reveal a slowly increasing number of women. An MBA is often regarded as a career passport and so is a useful indicator about the situation for women. In 2011 40 percent of the intake on the Ashridge one-year MBA program were women.

Global MBA Rankings of the top 100 MBA programs are published each year by the *Financial Times* newspaper.[47] In 2010 the number of women students was around 40 percent, having risen from 15 percent a few years previously. A survey from the Association of MBAs (AMBA)[48] in the same year puts the figure slightly lower – an average of 31 percent among all AMBA-accredited schools worldwide.

A similar upward trend is evident at Harvard[49] where women are now just over a third of MBA candidates accepted but back in the mid-1970s it was significantly lower, at 11 percent. This is a considerable change from the early beginnings of European MBAs when in 1968 there were only 4 women among a large class of 192 students![50]

WOMEN AND THE BUSINESS SCHOOLS

We can also review what's happened for women in business schools. The number of women faculty, the number of women who hold the top posts and are leading business schools either as deans or on the board and the number of women attending executive education programs, usually nominated by their employer, are all useful indicators.

Over the years at Ashridge we have seen the number of women delegates increase slowly and it now is just over 30 percent (on our open enrolment programs). Some other business schools have higher participation levels – the range among the top five (of 50 schools) included in the *Financial Times* 2011 annual Executive Education ranking is as high as 44 percent (in Spain) and as low as 17 percent (in Switzerland).

The number of women in faculty and on the boards of the business schools is also included in the FT Global MBA Rankings. One of the first women deans to lead a European business school was Professor Laura Tyson at London Business School – she held the appointment from 2001 to 2006. During this same period the number of women deans (the equivalent of a chief executive role) in the United States also increased. However, it was still not until 2010 with Sally Blount's appointment at Kellogg, Northwestern University, that a woman led one of the top American business schools. And, with a nice touch of history she became dean at the same business school where she studied for her PhD!

Women-only executive education

Women-only development is a topic that should be mentioned here, not least because it remains so controversial. Some see it is as an essential part of helping women leaders find their own confidence and to experiment and extend their leadership style. Others see it as divisive, as one person we interviewed said,

> *in the real world men and women have to work together so why have single-sex training for management development?*

There is not a simple gender split on opinions; women are equally likely as men in our experience to be critical (or supportive) of women-only programs and some people have no strong view one way or the other. Our opinion is that it can be useful and amazingly powerful. Ashridge ran a women's leadership program for some years during the 1990s and in recent years has run customized events in different parts of the world such as Abu Dhabi. Johnson & Johnson, BT (British Telecom), PriceWaterhouse Coopers, TimeWarner, IBM, Morgan and Stanley, McDonald's UK and the UK Civil Service have all offered women-only programs to help develop talented women who are either already at senior levels or in the pipeline just below.

THE CURRENT SITUATION

So, where are women managers – and is the glass half full or half empty?

There is a small group of women chief executives among the *Fortune* Global 500 companies[51] and while the numbers can hardly be described as significant, it's far better than the situation of say ten or even five years ago. The fact that the *Financial Times* newspaper published a list of the top 50 women in world business in 2009 indicates how much has changed. This was not something, as far as we are aware, that any European newspaper thought of publishing in the 1990s. http://womenatthetop.ft.com/articles/women-top/396bb974-f182-11df-8609-00144feab49a accessed November 2010. Similarly, *Fortune* magazine has, since 2005, published a list of the 50 most powerful women in business.

http://money.cnn.com/magazines/fortune/mostpowerfulwomen/2005/ full_list/index.html accessed November 2010.

If we compare women's progress to a journey then the situation for women leaders might well be described as travelling along a slow road with lots of bends, rather than a fast-paced journey along a straight, fast motorway. It is true that the number of women managers is slowly increasing in most countries. Unfortunately, the rate of progress is so slow that it is almost the antithesis to Moore's Law.[52] Instead of the numbers of women managers doubling every few years (which is what Professor Gordon Moore accurately predicted would happen over time for the number of transistors) we see instead a slow rate of change.

It's a point made in different sectors – such as Adelina Broadbridge's review of the retail sector.[53] Leonie Still[54] in 2006 wrote an article asking, 'Where are the women in leadership in Australia?' It's a question that might also be repeated in many other countries. In the UK a press article 'Are the British up to the chairman's job?'[55] in 2011 looked at nationalities of chairmen in the top 20 companies. The article demonstrated that it is also an all-male list; there are no women in this exclusive club. Another illustration of this is that the United States – accepted by many as being ahead of the curve in terms of progress – has very few female chief executives among the top 500 biggest public companies.[56] Yet as long ago as 1943 Tom Watson at IBM appointed Ruth Amonette[57] as the first woman Vice-President in the business. So why then is it taking so long for women to win through to the most senior executive levels?

The good news, and it is very good news, is that far more major employers take equality and diversity issues seriously, for example reviewing areas such as supplier diversity and working with schools and colleges to encourage non-traditional careers, etc. Similarly, many organizations now appreciate that there is a business case for diversity, something which was simply not true ten years ago.

However, most important is whether a business is concerned to create a culture which is more 'women-friendly' – something that might also be described as being more 'people-friendly' generally. Men as well as women suffer from the merry-go-round demands of working life, especially when this involves excessively long working hours, a pressured work environment and a punishing commitment for business travel. The high levels of stress that can be seen these days in many organizations are in part due to such unrealistic work schedules. The need for balance – juggling the demands of a fulfilling career with family issues – is important to both men and women, is a point emphasized in Accenture's 2007 review of women's careers.[58] It is a mistake to think that this affects only women. We think that organizations might do much more to review a creaky structure which requires senior staff to work such crazy hours. Some of those we interviewed say it's important to find a personal strategy for coping with such a demanding pace, whether or not you are a working parent.

SUMMARY

Back at the beginning of the 1990s few major employers took equality issues seriously. Views have changed significantly since then and many businesses now appreciate that promoting equality helps attract the brightest and best graduates. Another noticeable change these days is the number of senior business people willing to publicly champion diversity issues – Carlos Ghosn from Renault-Nissan and James Turley from Ernst & Young spoke at the 2010 Women's Forum held in France about the need for more women at the most senior business levels.[59] Another example is chief executive Chris Sullivan, an Ashridge governor, who has taken the lead at the Royal Bank of Scotland's UK and Corporate Banking Division as diversity champion.

There are four major issues for women in business today:

1. There are now more women at the so-called marzipan layer (an opaque level just below senior/director level that is difficult for women to break through). It is a critical mass in some organizations. The women are talented and hopefully we are beyond a time when appointments are made solely on gender rather than ability. (Some of this happened in the US to meet government affirmative action targets and invariably created hostility and resentment.) There is also greater social pressure on business to create equality in business at all levels. Will this create a tipping point for change?
2. There are more women managers with career ambitions than was the case back in the 1990s. Are organizations responding to this need with good career advice and support? Are men and women equally likely to receive key assignments or mentoring early on in their careers? How many organizations look at ways to ensure there is equality in such areas?

(Continued)

3. Another issue here is about the transition into a new job or promotion. Often individuals are given an opportunity but lack a mentor or coach to help ensure that they will succeed in the new role. Creating better support both for women and men taking on a new, demanding role would be a good investment for any employer. It's also an example of good talent management.

4. Many women (and many men) are working parents who also want to have a career. Earlier generations of senior women were often single and without children but this option is not what many women of today want. They expect that they should be able to have both a career and a family. There are far more dual-career and dual-income couples who find it extremely hard to juggle their lives. Few organizations are using flexible working, part-time options and career breaks in ways that support career development. Flexible working is simple common sense that should be available almost everywhere rather than something provided only by progressive employers. Legislation is not in our view the answer as this is unlikely to change attitudes within organizations. Employers need to find better models that will work for both the organization, across all senior roles and also for working parents.

5. Not every organization or chief executive understands that diversity is a business issue. The situation differs by sector although in some cases companies which are taking the lead on diversity stand out among their peer group:

> *I'm so pleased that I work for this organisation as we are light years ahead in terms of what we do to help women and to promote flexi-work. We can work almost from anywhere, anytime. When I talk to other people I hear real horror stories; the property sector for instance is back in the dark ages. Unless you are there in person in a suit with a clipboard you can't possibly be working.*

Interview quote

However, another commented that

> *It's still a bit of an old boys' club here.*

Survey quote

The next few years are critical for women's progress. Will it get better or will progress stall or, worse still, decline? There are plenty of talented women who should take their rightful place as business leaders. Positive interventions and structured support from employers are key components for success, so let's return to where this chapter began – why should business bother with equality? We'll leave the last words to one of our interviewees:

The teams that I've worked on that are more balanced, more diverse in terms of gender, culture and experience, have invariably delivered better results and created a great team environment to work in with a good degree of challenge and support, and importantly become places that others want to come and work in.

3

EARLY CAREER ISSUES

Looking back at my early career I didn't realise how important it was for me – I was meeting some great people and forming some strong bonds with individuals; some of these became the strongest friendships of my life.
Interview quote

This chapter deals with the importance of early career issues for working women. As the quote above illustrates, the value of what happens is often clearer when successful women leaders reflect on the early phase of their career. Of course, not everyone dreams of having the top job and being chief executive or chairman of the board. Some of us may wish to be teachers or scientists by choice or perhaps don't have any particular career dreams, but are happy to find a job we enjoy and stick with it whether as a manager, a professional or something else. That's OK and there's nothing wrong with that. However, there's always value in reflecting on your working life so far to help you understand more about your career and job needs. This can then assist and inform future choices and opportunities.

Our research shows that what happens in the early career phase can make a significant difference. It's hardly surprising that in the same way that the choice of university or topic studied can open or close certain doors, this also is true for the choice of employer, the type of job selected and what happens in those early years. In this section we reflect on what the women interviewed for this research say about their early career, the data from our survey findings, and why the issues identified are important.

Three key issues are evident in the interviews:

1. **Early opportunities**, perhaps the chance to take on a key project or gain valuable work experience. Often the value of this is something that the individual does not appreciate until much later.

2. **Help from others**, this may come from a boss or someone else in the company who acts as a good friend and advisor. They offer guidance and often see qualities that the individual is not yet aware of.

3. **Aim high**, a number of the women we spoke to say that they could and should have been more ambitious with their career plans. As one senior woman said her advice to younger women managers is *'go for gold.'*

Each of these headings is considered below. But there is also a fourth issue that we would add to the list:

4. **How do people get on around here?** The final section of this chapter considers career structures and pathways in organizations. It also touches on some career values and self-awareness questions such as 'are you doing the job you want to do?'

It is worth first pausing to reflect whether gender is an issue in discussing early career experiences. It is easy to see that each of the four points raised above would be relevant for both men and women. However, we think gender does make a difference and we briefly review below how the issues can differ for women. It's a selective rather than exhaustive list and we hope it illustrates what can go wrong for women.

Early career issues and gender

Early opportunities	Women can be less likely to promote themselves and, although this does happen for some men, it is important that organizations ensure women are as likely to get those early breaks, key projects or challenging assignments.
	In some organizations key career choices happen at key life stages. This is particularly relevant for younger women where those taking a career break may miss out. Recognizing these issues and helping ensure women stay in touch and are welcomed back after a career break is critical.
Help from others	An encouraging boss or someone else who sees their potential and qualities that the individual has not recognized in themselves. Many of the women we interviewed can pinpoint a boss, a mentor or supporter, often many people along the way, who helped them. They describe how this encouraged them to aim higher than they would otherwise have done.

(Continued)

31

Reality versus rhetoric in terms of diversity. Some organizations pay lip service to diversity but don't bother to look at what blocks women's careers in the organization or what can be done to overcome such problems. One organization has a 'career watch' for minority staff – this could also be introduced for gender.

Every good chief executive takes care to stay in touch with their younger generation of managers. Making sure they also understand what happens for women – and especially to those 'who disappear through the cracks' – could make a significant difference to women's progress over the next five years.

Managing a young family and a demanding job is rather like trying to square the circle. But let's be clear about this – it is not simply a women's issue. It's something which is true for men and women alike. Much more positive help for working parents would reduce the growing problem of 'burn out' and stress that happens in many organizations today. It's often practical simple changes that would help. Expecting people to travel at short (or no) notice is one issue. Another is absurd meeting times.

As one woman director said, '*I'm the only woman among 20 directors. All the rest either have no family responsibilities or have someone to take care of them such as a wife who doesn't work. So, when there are meetings early or late after 5 p.m. I am the only one who because of childcare issues finds this a problem.*'

Rosabeth Moss Kanter wrote in the 1980s about individuals who feel isolated, the minority person who is disadvantaged. She called it being an 'O' among a group of 'X's* and highlights how uncomfortable it is for whoever happens to be 'O'. It is clearly still an issue today.

Aim high

A number of organizations find women less likely to apply for promotion and are more content simply to do a good job. This factor may partly explain the gender differences in pay (and often in bonus) evident in different countries and sectors. Amongst a group of MBA students tracked from the University of Chicago the women earn less and the gap increased over time.**

Another issue is that some women believe that simply doing a good job is sufficient to get noticed.*** It is not. Career progression rarely happens like that and instead they may be overlooked and comments may be made at review time such as '*she's happy doing that job*'; '*she won't want promotion*', statements which are rarely checked out with the individual!

(Continued)

How do people get on around here?	It's often the case that women are not as likely to get the early breaks, the mission critical projects mentioned above that look good on their CV. This may happen because projects are assigned informally; people often talk about being 'in the right place at the right time.' Organizations could improve the situation such as setting up an on-line bulletin board to advertise current opportunities.
	Stereotypes also impact on women. As one person said, *'women have to work harder than men and have to prove themselves and have to continuously demonstrate their abilities'.* There's an issue too about management and gender – *'it's assumed that men will be good managers but women have to prove that they are.'*
	Too much of the career process and succession planning still happens informally and this invariably disadvantages women and other diversity groups. Career advice may happen for some but not for everyone.

*Rosabeth Moss Kanter: Being the 'O' in a group of 'X's, Times online article, 6 September 2007. There also is a DVD, The tale of 'O' – script by Rosabeth Moss Kanter and Barry A. Stein. Stein, B. A. (Producer), & Miller, J. (Animator) (1993). *A Tale of "'O'": On Being Different.* [Video]: Melrose http://business.timesonline.co.uk/tol/business/career_and_jobs/article2398505.ece

**'MBAs and pay: Female MBAs tend to earn less than their male colleagues', *The Economist*, 11 May 2009. Accessed June 20, 2011 www.economist.com/node/13271726

***Lois Frankel talks about 101 unconscious mistakes that women make which sabotage their careers, including 'no one is ever promoted purely because of hard work'. Nice girls don't get the corner office, 2010, is published by Hachette Book Group. It's a great book for exploring the behaviors that trip women up.

ISSUE 1: EARLY OPPORTUNITIES

Early opportunities can make a big difference for building a career profile and also for confidence and self-esteem. The chance to take on a major project or be a member of a successful and high-performing team can be a really good start to a career. This is not the solo model where an individual is given a task and with limited resources or advice is sent off alone to do as best as they can. What we mean is a far more positive framework with sufficient support and help so that the individual may be taking on significant challenge but they are not expected to do this alone.

Illustration: Career support

In one organization a few years ago women were being promoted to key roles – such as being the first female country manager. If they failed then this seemed to indicate that women (as a group) weren't capable of holding these crucial jobs. The organization wanted to ensure the women could succeed and so provided a job coach, someone with key knowledge, who could work closely with the women taking on these jobs and help ensure they were successful.

It's a really good idea for any new appointment. Some readers may say this approach adds significant costs for the business, especially in cut-back times such as these when everything has been scaled down. But think of this from the opposite side, there are costs involved but far less than the cost of a talented manager (either man or woman) who fails in a new post. If 99 percent of all new appointments were successful instead of 70 or 75 percent this would represent a good investment.

One critical incident mentioned by a number of the women who completed our survey is the opportunity of joining a high performing team or taking on a project that's important to the business. These opportunities are rarely something individuals ask for – it may happen by chance or because a mentor or a good boss understands how valuable it will be for the person concerned. The term 'stretch and challenge' is a good way of describing what happens; the individual learns different skills and begins to appreciate that they are capable of more than they had previously realized. So we might expand the phrase 'stretch and challenge' slightly, to 'stretch, challenge and support' as this then emphasizes the value of helping individuals given such opportunities. When this help isn't available people may feel they have been offered *'a liability'*, *'a poisoned chalice'* or it's *'work that means probable career suicide'*.

It is evident from our research interviews that many of these opportunities emerge through personal contacts rather than being provided in a more formal way by organizations. We think it is an area where organizations could do more to identify good early career experiences that will later help ensure the business will have the right skills for senior executives, and to create a structure to help ensure women have such opportunities. There could also be a great role here for professional networks to provide cross-company projects e.g., an online career opportunities bulletin board by professional associations which offers, say, a one month secondment for individuals starting out on their HR career to do a project at another organization.

Illustration: Early exposure to key projects

This was the first phase of my career. I've always worked for American companies and my career broadly falls into three phases – each with a different employer. When I joined the company on a training programme I was in my early 20s fresh from college and it's a very influential part of your life although you don't appreciate this at the time. The type of work I did and the discipline, the sense of urgency that was instilled in me at that time, laid a very good foundation for the rest of my career. I learnt how important it was to deal with problems very, very quickly which in the financial services environment where IT is critical this was essential. You have to be a good fixer. The firm was losing money if the IT stopped working; that creates a high-stress environment and it really concentrates the mind as well. I also learnt how to remove conflict quickly from a situation but in a positive way that still ensures you can get the job done.

Interview quote

Another person talked about doing a stint in consultancy after she took an MBA in the United States:

This enabled me to get lots of exposure to strategy projects and I built a great deal of expertise that in a single organisation would have taken me much longer to gain this.

Interview quote

Similar opportunities are also important later on in someone's career as the following example demonstrates.

Illustration: Standing in for the boss

When I worked in one company my boss really didn't like doing presentations and so he would let me do them. I didn't realise at the time, only much later, that it was a great opportunity for me to gain valuable experience.

Interview quote

What's striking about these early career experiences is that many we heard about – Gillian Hibberd, who is Strategic Director of Resources and Business Transformation at Buckinghamshire County Council, had the opportunity to conduct a major review on employee staffing – came about because a thoughtful boss recognized the value of providing such a challenge. The role of the boss is something that we'll discuss further in Issue 2, below.

> *As a very new manager, I went on an internal management training course. I complained to the trainer that it was unfair that I wasn't being given more responsibility and seniority. She told me to wake up and realise that no one 'gives' you anything; you have to prove that your bosses are missing an opportunity by not giving you more responsibility. For the next two months I did my job but highlighted, on a weekly basis, all the missed revenue opportunities that were there because I didn't have more resources and/or responsibility. Within two months I was promoted. It made me very aware that I am responsible for my own destiny.*

Survey quote

ISSUE 2: WHO HAS HELPED ME?

There are a variety of different sources of help available, as indicated in the table that follows:

Your boss	Colleagues
Internal coach	Internal mentor
External coach	External mentor
Family	Friends

As might be expected, the evidence from our survey – and from our interviews – indicates that most women use a variety of these sources rather than a single source (see the following table).

Survey question we asked: During your career please indicate the people who have supported you in achieving your goals

	Percentage*
Boss	87
Colleagues	77
Family	69

(Continued)

Friends	55
External coach (a relationship based on developing your skills)	33
Internal mentor (a relationship with a more experienced role model)	29
External mentor	20
Internal coach	11

*Respondents could select as many boxes as appropriate so each item could sum to 100 percent.

A good deal has been written about how earlier generations of women were held back by traditional – or conservative – management attitudes but this definitely is not true for the managers in our survey. For the majority of women their boss is a key source of career support – for 87 percent of respondents, followed by their colleagues, their family and friends. More than half of all our respondents are using one or more of these options. The pivotal role that the boss is playing in career development is striking – virtually 9 out of 10 women say that this helped them. We feel it's something that organizations need to be more aware of and ensure managers have the right skills needed for this role. One thought might be to ensure that all executive development includes a session on *'the role of the manager as career coach'*.

'**Organizational Tip'** – Ensure that all executive development includes a session on *'the manager as career coach'*.

Colleagues also are important to the individual but are often overlooked in career structures. Help outside of the organization from family and friends is mentioned by a significant number – 69 and 55 percent of respondents respectively. It's no surprise really to find many women turn to their family and friends – after all it's our nearest and dearest (usually) who know us best and more importantly are most likely to be candid and tell us the truth without holding back on anything! This type of advice, and perhaps also the encouragement we receive and their pride in us when we do achieve, can be another career multiplier. Lucy Kellaway, writing in the *Financial Times*,[1] notes the value of a supportive – rather than competitive alpha male – husband for successful women in business. One person we interviewed spoke of the continual demand of managing family alongside 'his and her' careers emphasized the partnership approach saying *'we're both in this together.'*

External career advice also provides a fresh view on what otherwise might be a closed environment – Hester Blaauw, who is Global Purchasing Manager at Merck, receives a lot of support and advice from her husband, *'I find it really helpful to hear the opinion of someone who is outside of the organisation. Because he is not involved in the business and he is good at thinking "outside of the box", he often comes up with good and practical advice.'*

Working for a large organization may mean more career support is available compared with smaller or medium sized companies but a word of caution, this is not always so, as one person explains – *'when I joined this new business unit HR said that there would be a feedback session after six months. This was forgotten about and only happened because I prompted them. It was not a standard procedure but depended on my initiative.'* **(Interview quote)**

Another example is where there are procedures that managers should follow for performance reviews – but whether these take place relies upon how conscientious and how busy the manager is. Managers however like Tang Fajin at Sinopec (see the illustration on page 127 – the manager's role in talent spotting) are crucial for identifying and encouraging younger, talented staff.

There is often a gender difference in that women are slower and/or more diffident than men to recognize their own abilities and this is one of the reasons why the role of a good boss can be crucial:

A coach and mentor are important but it's the line manager who is critical to your career. I've been very aware of this throughout my career and have often chosen a job because it gave me the chance to work for a good manager – you can change the job later, rather than focusing only on what the job is. My advice to women is that they should find good managers. It's so important for your career development.

Interview quote

Illustration: The manager as coach

I have been fortunate as I have worked for some really good managers – people who trust you and push you to do something that you're not sure if you are

> *capable of doing. They just say 'go ahead and if it doesn't work out then come back to me and we'll figure something out but I think you can do it, so try it out'. Having that kind of trust from someone you respect is really helpful and also the fact that they are pushing you beyond your comfort zone as you then find abilities you didn't know you had.*
>
> **Interview quote**
>
> *When we were looking at going into a new area my manager there pushed me to lead the project, which I would not have done otherwise. And it was a good feeling that wow, I was being trusted and people involved in the project listened to me and so I thought well OK maybe I can do this.*
>
> **Survey quote**

Too many organizations provide the 'challenge' part of the equation and don't provide enough (or sometimes any) 'safety net' to ensure people can achieve the task that they are set.

Mentoring and coaching are also used for career advice but less than the boss or colleagues. The focus on skills and competences in the way organizations use mentoring and coaching is probably partly why these roles have less emphasis on career development. Only 11 percent of respondents (see the table above) consulted an internal coach to help them achieve their career goals. This low response may reflect the fact that relatively few organizations use coaching – so this may be a role that could be enhanced. The coach or mentor can play a key role in talent management and with such good knowledge of the individual these are the people who know a lot about skills and leadership potential.

It's an area that organizations – and individual mentors and coaches – should review and improve upon. A new role, a 'career coach' could add value to what's already available in terms of career advice in many organizations. It would help individual women and an added benefit for the organization could be input into talent management discussions.

We also asked about help from outside the organization and the data reveal that an external coach is a more likely source of career advice – for 33 percent of respondents. External mentors are mentioned by 20 percent of respondents and can play a key role in career development – *'when I got a mentor – it was great, it changed my attitude and developed my self-belief.'*

ISSUE 3: AIM HIGH AND BE AMBITIOUS

Women should just go for gold – do what they really want to do.
Professor Dame Sally Davies,
Chief Medical Officer and Chief Scientific Advisor,
Department of Health and the National Health Service,
and Governor at Ashridge Business School.

Dame Sally Davies, one of the women leaders we interviewed for this research, believes that aiming high makes a difference and it's a view that many others agree with. It's not just having lots of energy and enthusiasm but it's about focus – decide what you want and go for it. Another woman talked about what often goes wrong:

> *Women always have a tendency to doubt whether they are capable and when they decide on university and if they have high university grades they still worry about 'can I do this or not', whereas men who are average or slightly above average are more positive and more likely to think 'of course I can do this'. I have always kept this in mind whether I'm negotiating a project or a new job – so my advice to younger women managers is that you can do it, so go for it!*
>
> *Instead of thinking of five reasons why you can't do something, think about why you can.*

Interview quotes

There are cultural differences around ambition as shown in the following quote. In the Netherlands, being ambitious has negative connotations, which made a complete contrast for one woman director compared to the people she met when she was away studying in the United States, *'where if you're not ambitious well who are you? But this really helped me decide what I wanted to do – well I like what I do and I want to be good at it, so let's go'* (**Interview quote**).

Illustration: Go for it!

One woman we interviewed who served many years on the board of a multinational recalls her earlier promotion to general manager. It was a competition with eight other excellent candidates and she recalls that at the time she felt very doubtful about her chances, so doubtful in fact that she probably would not have applied if it hadn't been for the fact that the general manager told her she should and that he thought she could do the job just as well as any other candidate.

> *The guy who held the job had put my name forward along with two of his team members. Until then I had been HR Director in one country but I didn't have a pure finance background which was unusual for these types of very technical roles, so this was a definite disadvantage for me compared with others who were in the running. I wanted the job but it was also a huge step up for me. However, the company wanted someone who could take on the change management/change leadership role and I did have that expertise. They took the view that I could learn the other skills and that among my team there was sufficient knowledge to ensure I would be well supported.*
>
> **Interview quote**

For another person it was external recognition – '*Winning the Personnel Today – HR Director of the Year was a great moment in my career.*' Another said,

> *Previously I have had some great bosses who could see my potential and encouraged me to try new things. It's back to the old question of what would you do if you weren't afraid?*
>
> **Survey quotes**

ISSUE 4: HOW DO PEOPLE GET ON AROUND HERE?

Sometimes it will be clear about what it takes to get on. Perhaps in one organization the need for operational experience is important, in another it will be a series of international stints. In, say, an engineering or technical environment those who aspire to a role at middle management level will need to demonstrate a high level of project management skills along with key technical/engineering experience. A universal issue will concern business contribution and as one woman said it's about understanding what makes you credible in the organization. It's often about meeting targets and delivering on budget – '*it's not optional, it's essential if you want to be taken seriously in any business*' (**Interview quote**).

However, there are often unwritten, unclear processes around careers in organizations and understanding these can help individuals

41

plan their own career. What are the key abilities, skills or attitudes that people need to get on in this organization? And of course how does your profile match the 'ideal' career profile? You may not need to tick every box on the list – some will be essential, others optional. Promotion boards and talent management reviews often happen behind closed doors and the individuals concerned are rarely given an opportunity to listen to what's being said about them or to correct misperceptions. Comments that might be heard about women were noted earlier in this section: *'she won't want promotion'*; or possibly *'she won't want promotion...yet'*; another might be *'she won't be able to re-locate'*. One survey respondent said, *'stop imagining what women want. Ask them – don't assume they don't want to travel, don't assume they don't want operational jobs.'*

One person interviewed recognizes such conversations and has heard many variations of these over the years: *'I've been involved in such discussions when these assumptions are made and that's why you may need a coach, you certainly need a mentor but you also need a sponsor – someone in the organisation who will take your part and speak up for you.'* Of course such a sponsor may also be a mentor or coach but her point is that sponsorship, especially in multinationals, plays a different and important part in career decisions. Sponsorship deserves to be more formally recognized. It's certainly something that individuals can think about – take a look at the simple career model, a career wheel, which is shown in the figure on page 43. At the heart of the diagram is **the boss** and personal **ownership** – *'be responsible for your own growth and development.'*

The two central supports are surrounded by other career supports. Tick how many of these are available to you and think about how the ones you don't have might help you. Think carefully about ownership – this refers to how much ownership you take for your own career. It's an obvious point to make but nevertheless worth saying that you need to be determined and take control of your own destiny.

I always had a goal ever since I started working. At first it was to reach the level my boss was on and to do this at a younger age than he had.

I was ambitious. Right from the start of my career I wanted to be a main board director by the time I was 30 – and I was!

Interview quotes

Reflective exercise – Career advice wheel

© Dent and Holton.

Career advice wheel

Most of the categories in the career advice wheel diagram above have already been mentioned in this chapter. However, business school alumni and networks have not been, and they are also valuable. Networks, both professional and personal, have helped a number of the women leaders we interviewed.

Networks and networking are now well-known phrases. However, the term is not something that everyone feels comfortable with, partly because some networking may seem superficial e.g., collecting as many business cards as possible at an event to see which will be of most benefit later to the individual concerned. Dame Sally Davies offers a different perspective. The term she prefers is not networks but alliances, which she describes as *'building friendships and alliances'*, and she makes the point that the word 'alliances' is different from networking, which is more often heard these days. *'I do network but the distinction for me is in the different relationship of alliances. It is a deeper relationship with someone who I respect and where usually we have shared values and interests.'*

It can also be harder for women working in male-dominated environments and a professional network such as the HR community available in the CIPD, the Chartered Institute of Personnel and Development, can be a great advantage. The IEEE, the Institute of Electrical and Electronics Engineers, a worldwide network for engineers, has a regular magazine and a number of women's groups based in different countries (for more information see www.ieee.org/membership_services/membership/women/index.html).

One woman interviewed recalls a time when another woman senior manager arrived in her business area – until then she had been the only woman at that level, *'don't assume that another woman will be a good ally. They might be, but they might also be a Queen Bee who sees other women as competition and therefore may be your worst enemy.'*

Business school alumni – another part of our career advice wheel – are invariably available to anyone who has attended a program, and networks are often established for specific programs. We are based at a business school and so must admit a certain bias in favor of such networks. However, we observe how useful both types of alumni can be for women managers. It's often harder for women to find a peer group – it's not always easy to join in at work if the social networks are a) mostly men and or b) revolve around golf, cricket, football and going out for a drink after work.

SUMMARY

Early careers should have plenty of help, support and direction and this will direct later progress. There is a faster pace of change these days in many organizations; people change jobs more regularly so it's important to be sure women receive first-class career advice and are not disadvantaged if a boss is not supportive. Working in a bigger business has some benefits for women. Hester Blaauw wanted to work for a larger employer as she felt this would provide more opportunities *'to grow my career so even if I stayed in R&D (research and development) I would have more opportunities to move around.'* Merck, where Hester works, is a leading Dutch employer, winning 'best employer' awards with its excellent reputation for looking after staff, providing opportunities to grow, etc. Additionally it has real credibility in the area of social responsibility – another quality which attracted her.

What are the key issues about early career experiences?

A good deal has been written about women's careers but most of this has focused on the mid-career phase. The evidence from our research highlights three issues. These have been noted before but in our view are important issues which can significantly help organizations be more successful with diversity:

1. Early career opportunities are just as important as those which happen mid-career.
2. Any organization serious about diversity needs to ensure such early career opportunities are made available in a more open, formal way (at present most happen on an informal, or ad hoc, way).
3. The roles of the boss and colleagues are important sources for career advice. How skilled are they for these important roles?

Reflecting on early career issues (see Chapter 9 for more about career planning)

For the individual

- What are your career ambitions for the next five to ten years? Think about where you are, the job you are doing and compare this to where you would like to be. Think about yourself as a brand (see Chapter 9 for more information).
- If you are offered promotion or a new opportunity think about how you can do it rather than about all the reasons why you can't!
- If you do not have a coach or mentor, find one. If you are based in a large organization also look for someone to sponsor you (it could also be the person who is your mentor or coach). A sponsor is a person who you feel will look after your best interests and help promote your qualities and abilities to the right people at the right time.

- Use your mentor or coach wisely. These people are not only capable of skills advice or to help improve your self-awareness but can also be a key source of career advice.
- Use any professional networks, university or business school alumni networks that are available to you.
- If you do not have a coach or mentor – find one. If you can't find anyone suitable then coach yourself.

For the boss/line manager

- Recognize the importance of projects which help broaden skills or offer opportunities to take on challenge.
- Look for ways to provide regular feedback to the women who work for you – make sure you don't save this up for an annual appraisal or feedback session. Regular feedback is especially important during the early career phase.
- Take time to discuss with staff what's important to them in their career longer-term and what they might do towards such aims.
- Encourage women in your department to identify their own mentor/role model.

For the organization

- A good deal of effort goes into attracting new recruits – are the same high standards maintained once people join e.g., do you survey new staff every few months to ensure that they have sufficient challenge, support and stretch in their role? How often do you offer career coaching sessions?
- Are men and women equally likely to be offered coaching during the early part of their careers?
- Are men and women equally likely to receive projects which will help them enhance their skill and build their confidence?
- Do you review the impact of diversity on your talent management programs? A survey by the CIPD[2] found that although most (81 percent) organizations did, the rest either did not, or did not know.
- Is flexible working available and if it is, is it regarded by employees as being career limiting?
- Every organization with in-house leadership programs should also have an alumni network to help participants stay in touch and network after the program finishes.

- Listen to women – *'talk to women in junior and middle management about what they want and whether they want senior positions.'* (**Survey quote**)
- How do you compare to what other employers offer – see the illustration below.

Illustration: Company best practice

An example of a good organization is one that provides lots of support, plenty of resources and help from the boss with a personal development plan. Think about your organization – how does it compare with the following multinational?

Personal development

We encourage our people to take advantage of the many opportunities for personal development and advancement. We provide processes, tools and culture to help you drive your personal and professional development and reach your full potential.

Those who take responsibility for their own advancement are supported with the personal attention you might expect to find in a small company, as well as the resources and commitment available in a large company.

To supplement on-the-job development, we offer extensive, easily accessible training and development resources. You and your manager can draw on these resources to prepare your personal development plan, PDP. Offerings include,

- Global leadership profile
- E-University
- Learning and development programs
- Leadership development programs

Global leadership profile defines the critical behaviors that characterize and establish effective leadership at all levels of our organization. This framework serves as a means for self-assessment and supports effective discussion between employees and their managers.

E-university provides online resources which may be specific to different regions or operating companies within the business.

Learning and development programs include training for new managers as well as negotiation skills, influencing, leadership development and

(Continued)

> a program to help staff align their personal goals with those of the company.
>
> **Leadership development programs** offer staff who have joined recently an accelerated development experience. These are led by senior functional staff and include two-year assignments which provide an opportunity to work across a range of different business segments.

Anyone based in a medium or smaller organization may find it difficult to compare their own situation with the multinational example provided above. Think about a few simple questions:

Do you offer lots of opportunities for personal development? For example think about how many job swaps and job shadowing opportunities have been available in your business over the past three months.

Do your managers have good coaching skills? For instance do you offer people training to develop their coaching skills?

Do you provide support, advice and encouragement to help women? Are women encouraged in your business; do they receive as much support as men? What about women balancing work and family commitments? Is the business flexible or inflexible? Do you ask women how the business could help provide a more women-friendly environment?

Your early career: 10 Tips

ONE Know yourself	Understand what are your strengths and key areas – especially in regard to leadership skills – that you need to develop.
TWO Improve your people skills	One aspect of this is the need to be a good communicator. Others are your ability to manage, develop and coach others.
THREE Plan your career – now!	If you don't have a career plan – sit down and write one now! What happens in your early career makes a difference so sit down and set out your plan; look at the next 18 months – 2 years; also think about your goals for 2–5 years' time (see Chapter 9).
FOUR Aim high	Be ambitious when you set your goals. It you don't hit those objectives you may be slightly disappointed but that's far better than setting your sights too low and regretting this later on in your career.
FIVE Mentors, coaches and most important of all, a sponsor	Find a mentor, find a coach and above all else, find a sponsor in your organization. A sponsor is someone who looks after your interests – they may also be your coach or mentor.
SIX Talk to your boss	Sit down and talk about your current performance and your future in the company. Discuss your career goals and ask for support to gain the key skills that are going to make a difference.
SEVEN Volunteer	Don't confuse this with simply asking for more work; it's all about opportunities. Volunteer for key projects and take the time to find out what opportunities are likely to be coming up in the next few months.
EIGHT Networking	Network and build alliances with people inside and outside. Join a professional network and the women's forum if there is one in your organization – if not think about starting one.
NINE You as a career brand	Think of yourself as a brand and sell yourself. If you don't do this why will others do it for you? See Chapter 9 for more about this.
TEN Reputation	Build your reputation and get a name as someone who is reliable, influential, leads others and above all meets targets. Think about this within your organization and externally as both can help.

4

CAREER PROMOTERS

Believe in yourself – even if people tell you it will be difficult, believe that you can do it.

Survey quote

Getting on in business and building a successful career takes more than hard work and a little bit of luck. We surveyed hundreds of women and one of the questions we asked them was 'What has helped you to achieve your career goals? List up to three things.'

We hoped that we would identify a few golden nuggets that we could share with you as areas to focus on. But careers are not like that – what we found was a huge variety of promoters that our respondents believed had helped their achievements so far. Many of the promoters that were identified were repeated time and time again by different women. These are the key areas women should take account of when building their career.

Career promoters

We have categorized the career promoters into the following areas:

- Personal Work Attitude
- Supportive Family and Friends
- Organizational Support
- Development and Developmental Relationships
- Self Awareness
- Opportunity
- Networking and Building Relationships
- Positive Working Environment

PERSONAL WORK ATTITUDE

Attitude to work is one of the key features identified by women for career success. It was by far the most frequently mentioned promoter of success for women leaders in business. Attitude to work comes in many guises from adopting a hard work ethic, to resilience or the ability to bounce back from adversity.

Hard work and a willingness to put in the hours, travel the miles, take on work others avoid and deliver excellence is important, though as one woman put it *'fear of failure – I have never meant to do well, I've always just wanted to avoid doing badly.'* For many, going the extra mile, working harder than those around them, multi-tasking and some-times breaking the rules when needed is what's been required of them. Many of the stories we heard from the women we interviewed also indicated that this hard work may also lead to certain sacrifices – some talked about staying single, marrying late, not having children, *'sacrificing personal time during the working week'* and being willing to move to new places to take up opportunities.

Determination and drive, aligned with ambition and a clear idea of the direction you want to go in are all cited as supportive of achievement. Having the persistence and perseverance to *'stay with it despite setbacks,'* which includes dealing with antagonism and discrimination. Also cited was the more positive aspect of determination where it was more about growth, learning and focus thus staying on track and achieving goals. People talked about taking on new roles and responsibilities and actively seeking new opportunities to build confidence and develop new skills. Determination and hard work were by far the most frequently mentioned personal attitudes in response to the question, 'What has helped you to achieve your career goals?'

The next cluster of important attitudes that was mentioned frequently includes self belief, confidence, passion and ambition. Self belief in the context of being able to do what you set out to do, having pride in your achievements, *'not being afraid to speak up and put across my point of view,'* believing that you are doing the right thing and being willing to take calculated risks. Self belief was often linked with confidence and expressed as belief in one's own ability and competence. *'The belief that I could do anything, and constantly reminding myself no matter how tough it got I could achieve whatever I wanted. This also meant building my self confidence which was a huge challenge'.* Passion and ambition also seem to be important – many women talk about the passion they have for their jobs, their own development and their personal ambition to do well in their profession or organization. It would certainly appear from the research and from our coaching experience that finding a career that excites, challenges and energizes you is a clear advantage over simply doing a job. Women also talked about the importance of being able to work in an organization and role that reflected their own values.

Less frequently mentioned but important nevertheless were patience, optimism, internal motivation, courage and commitment: For example, patience supported by a strong will and commitment to one's values, beliefs and career goals to wait for the right opportunities to present themselves; courage in the sense that women indicated that they often had to have the courage to take on opportunities and roles that stretched and challenged them; and the optimism, internal motivation and personal faith that they can do it.

REFLECTIVE EXERCISE

You may like to reflect and evaluate your own personal attitudes towards your career (1 being not like me and 5 being really like me)

Personal attitude	Self evaluation				
Hard work	1	2	3	4	5
Determination	1	2	3	4	5
Self belief	1	2	3	4	5

(Continued)

Personal attitude	Self evaluation				
Confidence	1	2	3	4	5
Passion	1	2	3	4	5
Ambition	1	2	3	4	5
Patience	1	2	3	4	5
Optimism	1	2	3	4	5
Internal motivation	1	2	3	4	5
Courage	1	2	3	4	5
Commitment	1	2	3	4	5

Are there any other attitudes you believe represent your approach to your career? List them below.

During this reflection and evaluation are there any attitudes you believe you could develop to help in your career progression? List below.

On reflection what personal attitudes do you believe have contributed to your success so far?   List below

How will you continue to capitalize on these?

SUPPORTIVE FAMILY AND FRIENDS

Guimei Pan, Vice President of Sinopec, recognizes the impact of life outside of work and talks about how important her family has been in helping her achieve at work, *'I never thought much about this during my career but looking back I can see how much the family have tried to help and support me. I have always wanted to be a dutiful daughter to my parents, my parents-in-law and in my own marriage I wanted to do my best, for instance helping my daughter in her education'*. She also knows that her husband and her family try to ensure she has the time to focus on her work commitments, *'they have tried to save me from some of the troubles that I might have worried about'*. Her father had been a factory manager and perhaps this helped as he had a good understanding of the pressures and demands that his daughter faced.

It goes without saying that for many of us we could not achieve our career goals without the support of our family. After hard work and determination having a supportive family and friends was by far the most frequently mentioned. Husbands and partners were particularly highlighted while other family members were mentioned but less frequently.

Parents were often mentioned as role models or of particular importance in providing encouragement in the early days of education and the first jobs by instilling a work ethic philosophy. Catherine Warne, Entrepreneur and Chief Executive of Red Door Communications, cites her father as one of her great supporters and says *'My dad always encouraged me to follow through my dreams rather than just stick at something for the sake of it ...'* In addition to moral support, parents also provide childcare and many working mothers indicate that without this support they could not achieve success. Close friends can also play a role and become informal coaches, acting as a sounding board and providing moral support when necessary.

For many of the women in our survey they cited their *'supportive husband or partner'* who provides emotional support and encouragement as well as sharing responsibility for childcare and household duties. In some cases the husband was actually the main partner responsible for childcare and had made the decision to take a different direction from the norm and either stay at home, work from home or work part time.

It appears from both our interviews and the questionnaire results that the support of family and friends has a major benefit for women achieving their career goals. Encouragement from family members while at school, college and in early jobs helps to establish a woman's confidence and self belief which helps to spur them on to deal with any challenges they encounter along the way. Supportive partners and friends also feature strongly, often acting as sounding boards and confidantes throughout many women's careers. Quite a number suggested that without these quality relationships they may not have managed to get to where they are today.

ORGANIZATIONAL SUPPORT

Line managers, bosses and senior colleagues seem to be the key here. Many women mentioned the support they have had from a boss (often a man) for giving opportunities, being encouraging, providing challenge and stretch assignments. They also mentioned being allowed to fail and learn from mistakes, provided these mistakes are then turned into learning experiences. Comments like *'working with an inspiring boss who gave me early opportunities to try new things out for myself'* were common.

It seems that the relationship element of organizational life far outweighs the provision of formal policies and practices that support working women. There was some mention of supportive organizational cultures where equality was encouraged but it certainly did not seem to feature as a career promoter.

DEVELOPMENT AND DEVELOPMENTAL RELATIONSHIPS

The role of education featured heavily as one of the major areas that supports women in their careers. Getting it right early on by having a good educational background, being willing to study for more qualifications (Master's degrees and MBAs were frequently mentioned) and as one woman states, *'a willingness to undertake further formal study to get where I want to go'*. Others cited that being involved in continuing professional development, gaining professional qualifications and *'focussing on my own personal development'* were also important.

However, it's not just about getting the qualifications; it's about how you use them. It certainly isn't sufficient to have a string of qualifications and a list of personal development experiences, rather it's about *'translating learning, knowledge and experience and putting yourself out there'*, and as another woman put it *'leeching all colleagues for what they can teach you'*. While formal qualifications play a role they are not the only element of development; informal learning and development on the job and ultimately putting it into practice are equally important.

Success for many women was helped by the developmental relationships they had with coaches, mentors and role models. Coaches who pushed them beyond their comfort zone and encouraged them to take on challenging projects provided an independent view point and a safe and supportive environment were mentioned. For many the coach helped them through a career transition and one woman commented that *'my external coach helped me to become more marketable within the organisation'*. Some women mentioned becoming a coach themselves which then provided them with a different opportunity to continue developing, by helping others develop and coincidently raising their organizational profile at the same time.

Mentors differ from coaches in that they are regarded as trusted advisers who will provide honest, practical guidance and also share their experiences with you. A mentor was often identified as the boss, line manager or in some cases a senior manager from another part of the business. Role models were mentioned as people you can look up to, people who provided inspiration and people with an outside perspective. These people were not always other women as one woman put it: *'watching and learning from senior staff, both men and women, around me'*. Recognizing the importance of this observational role early on in one's career appears to be of value in helping people to make their own decisions about the most appropriate behavior to adopt in various interpersonal work situations. Sam Smith, the chief executive of finnCap, recognized this in a recent interview in the *Sunday Times* when she talked about *'learning a lot about what not to do by watching people'*.[1] For one woman in our survey, learning from role models meant *'observing how senior colleagues acted in meetings when I was in a more junior role – bag carrying almost!'*

Illustration: Learning from observation

... Not having completed the theory of management by having the luxury of a university education, I learned from watching others. Most of the time my greatest learnings were from observing 'what not to do' from senior managers as I observed the negative fallout. However, I also try to mimic excellent behaviours.

Survey quote

Illustration: Learning from colleagues, peers and senior role models

A few key colleagues, peers and senior role models (although not formal mentors or coaches) have really challenged my thinking on my self perception and developed my self awareness which has been a life saver in so many ways. There are often times I doubt my own performance and I question the value I bring to an organisation. Over time I have learned to tap into and deal with these feelings and use them to propel my career rather than seek support for reassurance alone.

Survey quote

As mentioned earlier in Chapter 3, people who provide you with developmental opportunities are vital for your success and progression in a job or career. In many cases having a great boss early in your career who can then turn into a coach or mentor was invaluable to future career success. This sort of long-term relationship enables real levels of trust, honesty and openness to develop which leads to a truly worthwhile developmental relationship.

Gillian Hibberd says that *'people definitely have been the most important part in my career and they have inspired me. I consider myself incredibly lucky to have worked for some inspiring people – some of the best people in the business. My first boss at Oldham Borough Council – Fred Smith– was a great influence'.* Gillian's bosses at both Hertfordshire County Council and at Hackney are respected in the field of HR and have been mentors, and friends, to her. A key decision point at Hertfordshire was whether to return to the Assistant Director of HR role after her maternity leave. Her boss at the time encouraged her to return and to look for new ways of working once she did get back, *'without his support I would either have requested a part-time role or taken a step back in my career to another role; it would have been a tragedy. At specific points in your career people like that are so important, they give you the confidence by saying "yes, you can do it".'*

SELF AWARENESS

A finely tuned awareness of self featured as one of the key areas for career success. Many of the women who completed our questionnaire and those who talked to us during the interviews mentioned this area as something they had learned early on in their working lives. They also recognized how important it was for career fulfillment and achievement to know what you want, how you perform and how you can improve to be even better.

Self awareness can be gained through an acute understanding of one's own strengths, weaknesses, values, beliefs and needs. For many this means engaging in and receiving feedback from others and then reflecting on, and evaluating that feedback in order to decide the best course of action.

Illustration: Importance of feedback

Firstly feedback is extremely important and by understanding what you could do better you really learn. Initially in my career I was very impatient, I still am impatient, but I think the key is that you stay around long enough to learn from the mistakes you make.

Survey quote

In order to develop this self awareness it seems it is important for women to have a clear plan of what you want to achieve and where you want to get to. Whether this is done by focusing on short term plans, *'setting personal goals, looking too much to the future seems to get me caught up but if I set smaller steps for myself to take along the way, it makes the climb easier'* or having a long term plan, as one woman put it – *'my personal created future (10 year plan)'* this seems to be about personal taste as there is not one clear idea of how best to do this. However, it is clear to us that to achieve you need a plan to follow. That plan can be adapted along the way but it appears that those people who have a plan to follow are better placed for success than those who leave it all to chance.

Illustration: Importance of having a career plan

Completing a Masters degree in learning and development (Action Learning) where I had to complete a career review. Doing this enabled me to see how my career had 'accidentally happened' versus being a self directed/managed process and experience. I am now aware that I have the power to choose (to a large extent) what I want to do, where I want to do it and how I go about this.

Survey quote

Knowing what's important to you, having a clear set of values and beliefs that contribute to your career goals and provide you with a barometer by which to assess yourself appears to be valuable for many women. Recognizing what you have achieved, how you have achieved it and what you still want to achieve will help you to plan your on-going career. Structure isn't for everyone but having some idea of where you want to go can certainly help you to achieve success. (See Chapter 9 for ideas about career planning.)

Having a career and job that is driven by values means for many that it is easier to identify the kind of role and organization they wish to work for. This undoubtedly helps with the career planning process. As one woman said, *'Being clear about my values which ensures I always find my work worthwhile, even if not always well-paid.'* However, this can be a double-edged sword in the quest to get to the top. Being value driven can mean that women make decisions that rule them out of the top jobs or even certain career paths as they don't want to compromise their career, work–life balance or personal values. (We will say more about this in Chapter 5 which looks at career barriers.) That said, one of the major plus sides to having a clear value driver is that it enables a person to show passion and commitment more easily if they wholly believe in what they are doing.

OPPORTUNITY

Taking opportunities when they are presented is backed by a range of additional elements. Some people see this as luck, being in the right place at the right time and seizing opportunities when they arise, are mentioned by about 30 percent of respondents. While it is interesting that so many women feel luck has played a part in their career success, there is also a dark side to this issue. In an article in the *Sunday Times* Jack Grimston[2] talks about recent research undertaken by the Institute of Leadership and Management where women's levels of ambition added to their worries about whether they would be successful in a new role, leading to feelings of self doubt. In our view, this may account for our respondents indicating that luck has helped them rather than seeing their achievement as part of a bigger career plan. So, luck is fine but just imagine how much better it would be if luck was aligned with career plans.

Illustration: Importance of luck

Just luck – being in the right place at the right time. Due to expectations from top management a person had to be presented for the job on short notice – no full time worker with equivalent qualifications was available, so I got the job

Being in the right place at the right time and knowing the right people. Being a female delegate from a multicultural background was exactly what my organisation was looking for.

Survey quotes

Moving regularly and getting international experience were mentioned by many as significant contributors to their overall success. They talked about their ability to be mobile (both internationally and nationally) and thus available to take new assignments as an important element in their career journey. For some it was something to do early on in their career, for others later and for a few it was a permanent feature. This element of women's career lives goes some way to challenging the old fashioned stereotyping in some organizations, where it is suggested that women aren't available to travel or take on international opportunities. For many this is becoming possible because of the increase in home working and 'stay at home' fathers. In addition to this is the changing nature of attitudes to work where in many families it is recognized that the woman is the main breadwinner and therefore it is sensible to support her career.

Seizing opportunities when they present themselves may be easier for the single woman with no dependents and for some this is a choice they have made in order to achieve career success. For other women who are in relationships and also those who have families and other dependents it's more likely to be about the quality of these relationships. Success comes at a price and as one woman commented – *'you can have it all – but just not all the time.'* Success in a dual-career situation depends on the people involved and their ability to be honest and open to the possibility that the woman may have the better career prospects and to be willing to plan how the family as a whole will deal with this. Communication, openness and trust are vital here.

Illustration: Moving regularly

Moving jobs every three years, not necessarily companies, and sometimes sideways rather than a promotion. This broadens experience, fosters new ideas and provides new challenges.

Changing jobs frequently (at least once every two years) to work in larger organisations and gain experience in tackling a range of complex issues, and build a track record in delivering increasingly nuanced solutions.

Illustration: Working internationally

International experience has really given me a good grounding in the nature of organisations in different markets and different commercial climates. I have such a good feeling for how things work out in the field and back at head office. The cultural understanding and insights that you gain both working across a number of countries from a base such as London and being an expat means that you can bring a different perspective and ideas for success. I am also much more able to work with diverse groups of people and draw the best from them. It's fun too. For me I think it's just about doing what you like that keeps you engaged, international working is not for everyone.

Survey quotes

Taking opportunities when they arise has, for many, been the catalyst that was needed to build the confidence that anything is possible as long as you are willing to give it a go and work to the best of your ability.

NETWORKING AND BUILDING RELATIONSHIPS

The whole issue of networking has become increasingly popular in today's business world and the women in our survey are no different to men in this regard. While many simply mentioned it as an important element of gaining success others were more focused in their approach and described how they have targeted the networks.

Some of the things people mentioned as important include being proactive about the people you network with and the networks you join – for instance, belonging to and being active in your professional body which in turn gives you great opportunities to relate to others and build your visibility outside your own organization. Many women also recognize the importance of getting involved in strategic projects as a way of networking outside your usual sphere. This gives you the opportunity to build credibility, trust and also to impress key people who may be important for future career success: *'Impressing key people within and without the organisation. Those who will help me make connections for the business and personally'* also *'knowing the key people to watch and follow'.* There was certainly a trend towards proactive networking rather than just letting it happen.

The important thing to remember about networking is that it isn't simply about collecting business cards or lists of names on the various social networking sites; it is about making connections and building these relationships into useful contacts. People in your network do not have to be friends; the important issue with networks is to be aware of who you need in them and actively work to develop relationships with these people.

Networking exercise

Take a sheet of paper and develop a picture of your current network of contacts. It should look something like the following figure:

Network map

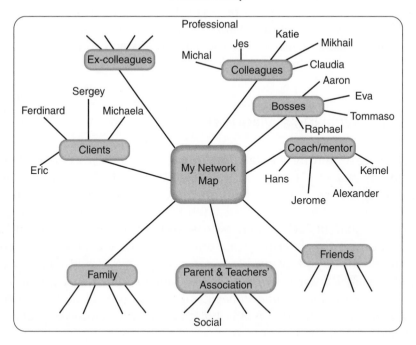

Now analyze it and ask yourself:

- How important are each of these people?
- What do I gain from each of the relationships?
- What do I offer to the people in my network?
- Which relationships do I need to put more work into?
- Are there any people who are missing from my network?
- How will I develop new relationships?

By understanding who is in your current network and keeping a track of the benefits and challenges in relationship networking, you can begin to understand more about who the key people are who will help you in your career development.

As one of our interviewees said, *'Be aware that the relationships that you form in the early stage of your career are the relationships that will help you later ... I didn't realise that until much later on in my career.'*

It will also highlight areas of weak relationships which may be worthy of development and help you to decide upon new relationships that are worthwhile developing. This may seem a little clinical but the more organized you are the better prepared you will be to take advantage of situations as they arise.

POSITIVE WORKING ENVIRONMENT

Choosing or finding the right working environment was mentioned by many women. For some it was down to luck that they found the environment that suited them and have thrived in it. For others they have had to seek out an environment that is supportive to women, that fits with their values and some have started their own business in order to create one. Catherine Warne is one such woman who says, '*I wanted to create a company that broke the mould and actually delivered what it promised. Senior people, senior consulting and excellence through and through*'. Of course, setting up your own company may not be possible for many of you. However, having a clear idea of the type of organization and working environment that appeals to you will undoubtedly help in your career development. You might also like to reflect about the qualities you would expect in the leaders in your dream organization. The leadership of any organization is key to the culture that permeates and will ultimately have a huge impact on your ability to enjoy, fit in and thrive in the organization. When one feels confident, valued and motivated in a job and organization then it is much easier to grow and develop.

We both believe that our own careers have flourished and we have been able to develop and grow in our jobs because we found an organization (Ashridge) that encourages individuality, use of initiative and autonomy. We have both worked for the organization for over 20 years and truly believe that women are equally valued for their contribution as men. In Fiona's previous experience in the financial services industry this was not always the case.

Having the right people around for help and support is good but getting the right organization and work environment can make or break a career.

As two of the women in our research noticed:

I find that people enjoy working with you more if you have shown them appreciation.

Interview quote

and

Working within a supportive environment, i.e. close relationship with my boss and mentor and close relationships with peers and direct reports - we learn together from mistakes and celebrate our successes.

Survey quote

Key messages for promoting career success

ONE Having a positive work attitude	Working hard, being determined, focused, motivated, committed to your goals and having an optimistic outlook all seem to contribute to career success.
TWO Recognize the importance of family and friends	Not just as support networks but also as role models, mentors and coaches.
THREE Finding the right organization	Working in an organization that supports and encourages women and men in equal measure, that appeals to your value system and also where you get support from your boss and colleagues.
FOUR Being self aware	Knowing what you want, what you are good at, what you need to develop and having a career plan.
FIVE Recognizing the importance of development and developmental relationships	Having the right education, whether this is formal or informal and being open to development and feedback. Having a coach or mentor who can challenge and guide you.
SIX Being prepared to take opportunities when they arise	For some this is simply being in the right place at the right time but for others this is about being willing to take a risk and having the courage to try something different.
SEVEN Proactively network and build relationships	Having a well-developed range of connections and contacts with whom you can have a mutually beneficial relationship.

5

CAREER BARRIERS

The things that have held me back are only my own fears and the choices I've made – some consciously and some unconsciously – no external factors.

Survey quote

What is it that hinders women in achieving career success? We asked the women in our survey to identify up to three things that they felt had hindered them. As illustrated by the above quote it appears that women continue to be their own worst enemies. The most commonly mentioned topics tended to focus on women's own self doubts and limiting beliefs (see the figure that follows). External areas and contributors were mentioned but with far less frequency than women's own personal frailties and commitment to their family responsibilities. So, while many barriers were identified, these were often cited as being choices that had to be made by the woman herself and therefore were career limiting for a while.

Career barriers

We have categorized these limiting areas into the following topics:

- Limiting Beliefs
- Family Issues
- Work Colleagues
- Personal Style and Skills
- Lack of Organizational Support
- Gender Issues
- Taking the Wrong Path
- Politics and Bureaucracy

LIMITING BELIEFS

This is by far the most commonly mentioned hindrance to a woman's career development, progression and success. Comments such as *'lack of confidence', 'lack of self belief', 'not pushing myself forward', 'thinking I'd not be good enough', 'self doubt', 'limitations I put on myself', 'low self esteem and procrastination'* feature regularly as one of the three things women mentioned.

It seems that many women blame themselves for slow progression or non achievement. Confidence (and variations on this) appears to be an issue for many women.

Illustration

I am conscientious and sometimes lack self confidence. I am happy with my career progression but sometimes wonder if I could have gone further quicker if I'd been more bullish or prepared to 'blag' it a bit more.

There are lots of reasons cited for this lack of confidence and for some it appears to be an inherent personality trait, such as modesty, introversion or non competitiveness. For others it is lack of feedback and support about their ability and therefore little reinforcement of their capability and performance. In general many women seem to find it challenging to promote themselves and have the confidence that they can move into a more senior position. Some of the other career barriers contribute to women's limiting beliefs and may reinforce the feeling of lack of confidence. That said, as was seen in

Chapter 4 once women have the confidence they usually find they can do the new job, hold their own in a boardroom and have the same, if not more impressive, skills than their male counterparts. The challenge seems to be getting women to recognize that they do have the ability.

FAMILY ISSUES

Organizations may have excellent family friendly policies in place but it remains clear from our study that a whole range of parenting and family issues serve as barriers to a woman's career progression and development. Most of the women recognized that decisions made in relation to family life required compromise and in the main it was the woman in the relationship who compromised, often out of personal choice. In this category reasons given include *'having a family', 'being a single mother', 'working part time', 'caring responsibility for child with special needs', 'having two babies in two years', 'family constraints meant lack of geographical flexibility', 'taking a career break', 'desire to be based near family members for support', 'not wishing to work long hours', 'caring for ageing parents', 'chose family first!'*

Paradoxically it appears that for many women their own personal choice in relation to their commitment to family life contributes to hindering their career progression at least for a time. Many women in our survey seem to accept this as an inevitable consequence of motherhood and their personal need to take responsibility and be there for their children.

However, there is another category where the family issues were illustrated as clear barriers to progression. These include *'blatant sexism-assumption that I would have kids at some time in the future', 'people being aware I was thinking of having a second child', 'being told I was very good at my job but I would not achieve anything because I would give up work when I had children – I nearly believed them!', 'chauvinistic partner/ husband, prejudice – promotion blocked after announcing I was pregnant.'* These barriers make us think; what has changed for women in business? They are attitudinal issues that will undoubtedly continue to be evident if unchallenged. The legal system and company policies and procedures can only go so far. There was certainly evidence from many women that speaking up about such attitudes would only make things worse. It therefore seems that for many women in business a vicious circle is in operation – their organization can point to their generous family-friendly policies but then the reality of day-to-day life is rather different with management offering little real support, flexibility or encouragement when women face the daily challenge of being a working mother.

This is a sad reflection on some organizations; undoubtedly many women's careers suffer from continued gender bias and businesses that allow this sort of behavior will lose good women to more enlightened organizations or they will opt for an independent or entrepreneurial career.

WORK COLLEAGUES

In this area there were three key themes emerging:

1. Poor line management often stated as managers taking credit, putting up barriers and bullies;
2. Other women who see you as a threat;
3. Lack of support and development.

First is the problem of having a poor or incompetent boss who is not supportive or more worryingly is actively unsupportive. Sometimes this sort of manager takes credit for others' work and actively promotes it as their own. Sadly the theme of the following comment was not unusual: *'Being bullied by my manager; this destroyed my confidence and made me feel I was not capable of performing well, despite being told other-wise by my previous manager.'* (**Survey quote**)

Aggression and 'macho' behavior remains a common problem according to our survey and interviews, by both male and female bosses and by colleagues – the use of intimidating behavior, often by people whom our respondents believe to be incompetent is one issue. It is particularly sad to hear about other women who 'bully' or block another woman's career. We heard several stories from women about this sort of thing happening; for example the following comments were typical of the stories we heard: *'bosses – particularly female bosses without children', 'a bullying female boss'* and *'more senior women who have blocked my progression.'* (**Survey quotes**)

One particularly unhelpful behavior cited was when a woman's career progression was blocked because *'my boss did not want to lose me from the organisation so did not put me forward for opportunities outside the business unit'.* Evidence of this type of behavior was all too common and allied with a woman's lack of self belief; it is clear that many successful women are not progressing as quickly as they might do if they were more self confident and if they had better quality feedback and support from HR, bosses and colleagues to promote their self confidence.

PERSONAL STYLE AND SKILLS

Physical attributes were mentioned frequently as a major career limiter: in particular age, stature and hair color! It appears that being young, short and blonde can all be a major disadvantage to career progression – *'being young, blonde and female has not always been helpful'.* Age was mentioned by many women as a hindrance, both being too young and too old – *'being older than the norm in my current organisation I was actually told when I applied for promotion a year ago that it was someone else's turn to start out on their 30 years in management!'*

Many women believe that their personal style has held them back, for some the need to please and being generally too nice are cited as career limiters. Comments such as *'my willingness to help out everybody all the time means I am perceived as more junior and less strategic'* and *'if I show the same assertiveness as men, it is perceived as harsh and rude'.* **(Survey quotes)**

On the other hand being regarded as outspoken, challenging, competitive, critical, serious, perfectionist and aggressive are all mentioned as personal characteristics women regard as career limiters. For instance, *'Not being enough of a chameleon. With me, what you see is what you get, that is not always the best approach. My forthrightness can scare people'* and *'During my initial years in the organisation, I was given negative feedback about my style, considered too assertive for a woman. I had to find a balance between the organisation's expectations and being myself to become more effective, and had to do this with little if any support.'* **(Survey quotes)**

Issues of influence such as an inability to recognize the importance of managing upwards, failing to follow up on own instincts and lack of communication skills were also mentioned by several as barriers.

Additionally, impatience, slow progression, being too practical and being kept as a strong number two were seen as blockers.

Creating a positive impression by developing an appropriate style to suit both the individual and the organizational environment within which one works, appear to be important for career success and progression. In addition to this, having key skills and demonstrating them effectively will undoubtedly be of benefit.

LACK OF ORGANIZATIONAL SUPPORT

While enlightened organizations offer support to their staff (both women and men) through coaching and mentoring systems, regular performance reviews, talent and succession management processes, it appears that there are still many places where organizational support is lacking. The major areas mentioned related to lack of or limited career opportunities within an organization, no coach or mentor and a lack of feedback.

Comments like *'lack of future opportunities within current organisation'*, *'there was no talent management within the company'* and *'longer established personnel in positions with no plans to move sideways or upwards'* all seem to indicate organizations with little realization of the importance of internal career development and promotion planning. Many of our respondents felt let down by their company when they found that career paths were not obvious, were sometimes blocked and little encouragement and opportunity was given to women who wanted to grow and develop. Some mentioned that plum jobs were given to men or 'favorites' rather than the best person for the job, others mentioned 'dead men's shoes' and others simply talked about lack of awareness of job vacancies until too late.

The lack of a coach or mentor was cited on many occasions and it seems that people who did not have such a relationship early on in their career found it to be a disadvantage later. Having someone who can challenge, support and act as a sounding board was seen as vital for career progression and development. Formal coaching and mentoring systems seem to be more common today; however, many women mentioned *'not having a coach or mentor early enough in my career and therefore didn't have a career plan'* or *'lack of guidance in the first 10 years of my career'* as serious career barriers. This suggests that it can be of significant benefit for women themselves to identify a coach

71

or mentor early in their professional lives. Perhaps the secret is not to leave it to the organization but to identify your own coach, mentor or role model.

Feedback plays a vital role in a woman's career development. Lack of it leads to lack of self awareness and self belief. As one woman put it, *'failing to obtain effective developmental feedback from colleagues and managers at step change points which delayed the next move'* and another said, *'being unsuccessful in applying for new roles but not getting anything concrete as feedback, so being unclear about reasons and development opportunities'*, the statements indicate that by not asking for feedback the women in question were hampered by their lack of awareness of what they could do to develop and therefore be more ready for the next career move.

Typically most working people get feedback under two circumstances:

1. When they have done something wrong or badly

and

2. During their annual performance review.

In both situations it is also common that the feedback is not particularly useful for growth and development. Asking for, and getting, useful feedback is down to the individuals themselves and in order to build a good level of self awareness feedback needs to come from various people – bosses, colleagues, reports, customers, mentors and coaches. Everyone will have a different perspective and all feedback is useful.

It seems that you cannot rely on the organization to support your career development; it really is down to you. As a first stage it is worthwhile getting into the habit of asking for feedback – not just in formal situations like performance reviews but in everyday situations. So instead of waiting for others to give feedback – you could wait a long time – ask for it. By identifying people who can help, in addition to bosses and colleagues – coaches, mentors, role models and sponsors you will be giving yourself a clear advantage and gathering data which can help you both develop and progress.

The key message here appears to be that some organizations do not overtly offer support to their people. Progression, development and feedback are all areas that the individual must take responsibility for. It is also worth saying that while our survey and findings relate to women we believe that many men may also have similar stories to tell in this area.

GENDER AND DISCRIMINATION ISSUES

Perhaps one of the most worrying barriers to a woman's development is the whole area of gender and discrimination. It seems that gender discrimination is still prevalent in this so-called enlightened age. It may be that it isn't as obvious but some of the stories we heard during our research indicated that gender discrimination remains a problem. It appears that no amount of legislation can change attitudes that are ingrained in decades of social conditioning.

Some of the comments we heard include *'as a woman not being heard by men at the top who have no insight into their behavior', 'overlooked in all male environments, boys club mentality still prevails in many parts of the civil service', 'male, pale and stale Exec boards', 'sexism', 'my lack of desire to learn golf'* and *'the old boys' network'*.

It does, however, appear that discrimination is now more attitudinal and more about behavior that continues in some environments, although some cultures were singled out for specific mention. These include parts of the civil service, academic medicine, the Church, engineering and manufacturing. Perhaps these attitudes also account for the fact that women are still in the minority in senior levels in organizations, and as the much publicized report 'Women on Boards' conducted by Lord Davies indicates,

Over the past 25 years the number of women in full-time employment has increased by more than a third and there have been many steps towards gender equality in the workplace, with flexible working and the Equal Pay Act, however, there is still a long way to go. Currently 18 FTSE 100 companies have no female directors at all and nearly half of all FTSE 250 companies do not have a woman in the boardroom. Radical change is needed in the mind-set of the business community if we are to implement the scale of change that is needed.

And one of the recommendations is,

> that UK listed companies in the FTSE 100 should be aiming for a minimum of 25% female board member representation by 2015.[1]

TAKING THE WRONG PATH

In hindsight one barrier that many women recognize is that they have *'taken the wrong path'* at some point in their career. For some this means choosing the wrong career right from the start, or being pigeon holed into a career due to qualifications or circumstances. For other women it involved staying too long in one role or with one organization or having experience in only one sector. Economic downturns also play a role with several women, for instance: *'graduating during a recession and taking jobs because I felt I had to.'* Redundancy was also mentioned as a reason for taking the wrong path either for staying in one place too long or, having being made redundant and taking a new job too quickly just to get back on the career ladder then discovering it is the wrong job or organization.

Misplaced loyalty was also mentioned, to a person or an organization. This led to women staying too long in one place and being overly dependent on that person or organization to recognize their talent and develop or promote them. Ultimately this can lead to derailment for the woman concerned as others could perceive her as lacking in ambition or overly reliant on the boss. It is important to understand that being loyal and working hard for the boss and the team are good qualities but it is also important to know when people are taking advantage of you. So, if you feel this is happening to you ask yourself whether the loyalty is a two-way process – is the loyalty mutual? Does your boss offer you development opportunities? How long is it since you discussed promotion or your career development? Do you feel your boss represents you fairly to others? If you have negative responses to these questions then you may be one of these women who is overly loyal and being taken advantage of. Remember it is up to you to manage your career development; no one else can do it for you. If you are happy with the current circumstances then so be it – this isn't a hindrance but if you are unhappy do something about it.

POLITICS AND BUREAUCRACY

Organizational politics are a fact of life in business. The issue for men and women alike is the level of politics that is prevalent in their organization and the degree to which any individual is willing to play this political game. For many of us we see politics as a negative and certainly many of the women in our survey saw politics as a major barrier to their success. Statements such as, *'my dislike of corporate politics'*, *'not playing the political game – especially with more senior female managers who expect more from females than males'* and *'office politics and people who stand in your way'* were typical.

Some women find office politics a complete turn off and they are unwilling to play what they see as the games that they believe are necessary to progress within their organization. This choice not to play the game can of course be a double-edged sword and they may find that by not working with the politics they can find that they work against them as several women indicated, and as one said, *'refusing to play office politics and break my principles'*. One way to change your attitude to politics is to frame it in a different way, for instance, by accepting that politics are a fact of life and simply one of the many interpersonal challenges one has to face day to day. Identify what you believe is a political situation and set yourself a learning goal to work with the situation and people involved in a positive way so that you can genuinely develop your political skills. Not all political operators are Machiavellian; many are simply astute leaders and influencers. As one person said, *'be savvy about organisational politics – they exist!'* (**Interview quote**)

In addition to office politics, bureaucratic processes also get in the way. For instance, *'the various HR rules the civil service has in place about needing to spend a certain amount of time in a grade before being eligible for promotion'*. Institutional red tape like this can get in the way and many women prefer to play by the rules until they realize that sometimes rules exist only in one's head and are often a result of custom and practice rather than being an actual rule to be obeyed. It is always worth challenging the rules or at least asking a question – what can you lose?

TIPS FOR OVERCOMING BARRIERS

1. **Understand what it is that blocks your career** – try completing the quiz that follows to help with this.

Exercise – potential career hindrances

Look at the list below and tick all of the items that have limited your career to date or could limit your career in the future:

☐ Not applying for a promotion due to lack of confidence
☐ I'm too valuable in my current role, so can't let them down
☐ I can't apply for a new job while the children are young
☐ I don't think my personal style will suit a managerial role
☐ I'm too young/old to move to a new role
☐ My qualifications are not good enough for the next level
☐ My organization will promote me when they think I'm ready
☐ I've been with my current organization too long I can't move now
☐ I've always worked in the public/private sector so can't move to the private/public sector
☐ I like what I do, I'm a bit bored but don't want to take a risk
☐ There's no point in even applying as a woman won't be promoted to that level in this organization
☐ The job involves a lot of travel, so they won't give it to a woman
☐ I can't let my boss down, he/she has always supported me so moving now would seem disloyal
☐ I daren't take the risk. I really enjoy my current job and would hate to move to a new role that I don't enjoy or can't do well
☐ I don't want to leave my current staff/team and let them down
☐ I have never been encouraged to apply for promotion
☐ My life is in good balance and I don't want to upset the balance
☐ I don't want more responsibility
☐ I don't want to be a role model
☐ My current competence and skill don't match the job on offer

Add in any others that you can identify:

Add up how many you have ticked: ☐

The more you have ticked the more likely you are to hijack your own career.
Being aware of the potential imitations you put upon yourself is the beginning of your journey towards change for the better.

2. **Identify people who can help you** – people who can provide you with good quality feedback about your performance. People who will be willing to challenge and support you to get on track. Support is great but you also need people to challenge you so that you don't fall back into negative habits.

3. **Develop a career plan** – if you don't know where you want to go how will you get there? See Chapter 9.

4. **Create an external perspective** – work with someone outside of your organization. Having this type of objective advice can often help you see situations more clearly.

5. **Manage your professional image** – take control of the impression you wish to make in business. Think about your behavior:
    - when you meet people for the first time;
    - when you attend meetings;
    - when you are with your boss;
    - when you are with your reports.

Remember:

Source: Dent and Brent 2010.

6

WOMEN AND LEADERSHIP

I am a coaching style of leader and I want team members to experiment and try out new ideas but I'm also very results oriented – I'm not soft.

Interview quote

Leaders exist at all levels in organizations and based on the data collected in our survey it appears that while women hold leadership positions they are under represented at the most senior levels. Recent research by Lord Davies indicates that nearly 50 percent of FTSE 250 companies do not have a woman on the board. In our research there was a definite feeling from over 60 percent of our respondents that men still have a better deal when it comes to getting into senior leadership positions. Like the Davies report, we found that lack of access to powerful informal networks was cited as one of the key reasons for this together with the ever-present issue of being a working mother. In addition to this many women felt that their leadership style was not valued or regarded as not tough enough for top leadership. The focus of this chapter will be on leadership style and will make some suggestions about how women could better prepare themselves for more senior leadership positions.

There are many definitions of and qualities attributed to good leadership; typically these include words such as – integrity, openness, humility, dedication, honesty, confidence, courage and compassion. All these words are appropriate and yet success is about how all these characteristics are deployed by an individual when leading others. We feel that the following two quotes capture the essence of leadership in the 21st century and resonate with our own views on the topic. *'No one has it all. It's a matter of fit. True leadership involves calibration of behaviour to fit a given situation'* (Hodgson and White, 2001) and *'Leadership is a social process; it happens between people'* (Binney, Wilke and Williams, 2005). For our research we wondered whether there was a leadership style favored by women.

As you will see later in this chapter it seems that on the whole women tend towards the more participative and collaborative leadership styles. However, this isn't the full story – many of the women in our research indicate that anyone who believes they are a push over will soon find that they are mistaken. While a woman's preference may be towards a more participative involving approach to leadership, when necessary many reported that they can flex their approach to make tough decisions, direct others and clearly state their point of view. It is important when considering the leadership role and women that you look at assigned leadership roles and also recognize those situations where leaders emerge, where they have no authority but might have knowledge, expertise or simply choose to take a lead – for instance when responsible for instigating major change in the organization or influencing others about a new project idea. As women in business it is important to recognize when you are in a leadership situation and not only when you are formally assigned the leadership role. This awareness will enable you to capitalize on and make the best of these opportunities. Many women told us stories about opportunities that in hindsight were great leadership experiences. It is not unusual to reflect after the event, but just think how much more effective you could be if you were more aware of the present and able to plan and think through the best approach to take and how such experiences could contribute to your future career.

Illustration: Early leadership opportunities

One story that illustrates this point is from one of our interviewees, Gill Collinson, who started her career in nursing. It is only in recent years that Gill has realized how important some of the early experiences were in relation to developing both her career and leadership skills. Following her specialist training in cancer care she moved to a large NHS hospital in the South East of England where she opened the first nurse-led chemotherapy unit in the UK. As she said, *'I did not know the significance of this (role) at this point'.* This experience led to other appointments as well as opportunities to present

(Continued)

at conferences and to take part in policy committees about cancer care. In hindsight Gill has realized how important that early leadership experience was for her career and in building and developing her confidence, skill base and reputation.

Later in this book we will look at career planning where we will offer ideas, thoughts and processes for making the most of your business and life experiences – past, present and future. Some of the ideas we offer will help you to be more aware of various situations that are developmental and how to capitalize on these in your current role and for your future development.

The remainder of this chapter will explore leadership style and how women can best focus the development of their style and approach for future success.

Leadership style

In our survey we asked women to describe their primary leadership style and gave them seven options. We selected these styles as representative of those that we hear talked about during our work at Ashridge. Undoubtedly there will be other ways of describing leadership style and behavior and this is not intended to be an exhaustive list, but simply a guide to those approaches that we believe many people currently use. The options were,

1. **Participative** – you actively involve others in discussion and decision making
2. **Situational** – you vary your style to suit the situation
3. **Visionary** – you inspire others through your energy and commitment
4. **Transactional** – you give directions and expect them to be met
5. **Value Based** – you lead based on strong personal values
6. **Intuitive** – a more instinctive approach where both people and the situation are considered – gut feel
7. **Hierarchical** – driven by level and status.

The results are as shown in the figure that follows:

Leadership style

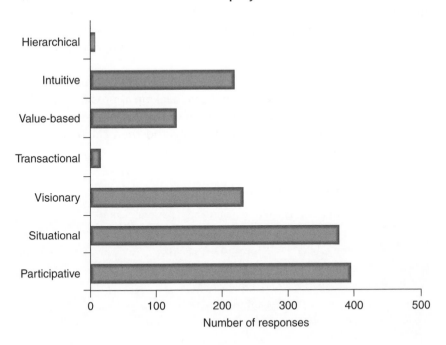

The results indicate that participative and situational are by far the most popular styles adopted whilst hierarchical and transactional are used by very few women. However, a number of respondents indicated that while they had a preference for one style comments like '*More than one style applies here*', '*A combination of many of the above*', and '*I think my style is a hybrid of participative, situational and value based*' were frequent. In fact many people indicated that they had a preference for a mix of participative, value based, intuitive and situational.

Leadership and leadership style is not an easy subject and much has been written about the topic. There is no one 'perfect' style, approach or theory. In recent years one theory that has become popular is described as authentic leadership. We suspect that there is some merit in this as most of us would like to be regarded as demonstrating authenticity in the way we behave towards and lead others. However, this does not help to describe our style preference as any one of the styles can be demonstrated in an authentic way, which we understand to mean being true to yourself and acting at all times with integrity and in a genuine and consistent way. We believe that by raising your awareness of a range of styles and developing your own particular use of these styles will help to contribute towards your success as an authentic leader.

As a starting point you may find the following questionnaire useful to help you reflect on your preference and back up approaches. Look at the chart that follows and indicate which of the phrases best describes your leadership style – mark all that apply and then calculate which style is your preferred style and back up style.

Participative Style Exercise

STYLE A	☐ I involve others in discussion and decision making
	☐ I build consensus with others
	☐ I use others' expertise and experience
	☐ I consider others' perspectives
	☐ I am open minded and encouraging
STYLE B	☐ I vary my style to suit the situation
	☐ I am flexible and adaptable
	☐ I analyze what's needed and adapt my style accordingly
	☐ I am conscious I use different styles
	☐ I take care to make people aware of my choice of style
STYLE C	☐ I inspire others
	☐ I energize and enthuse others
	☐ I like to present ideas about what could be for others to buy into
	☐ I present complex ideas by translating them into practical actions
	☐ I use novel ways to express my ideas
STYLE D	☐ I give concise directions
	☐ I expect others to carry out my requests
	☐ I am clear when communicating what I expect of others
	☐ I am confident making decisions
	☐ I take responsibility for getting things done
STYLE E	☐ I have strong personal values
	☐ I like to follow my principles and beliefs
	☐ I like to lead people who share my values
	☐ I am attracted to people who share my beliefs
	☐ I prefer to work in organizations that share my standards

(Continued)

STYLE F	☐ I rely on gut feel when leading others
	☐ My instincts drive my behavior
	☐ I use previous experience to gauge my leadership behavior
	☐ I make quick instinctive decisions
	☐ My sixth sense guides my leadership approach
STYLE G	☐ I am driven by level and status
	☐ I like to be in charge
	☐ I believe the most senior person should lead
	☐ Status is important to me
	☐ My senior position commands respect

The highest number indicates your preferred style/s followed by your back up style/s.

A. **Participative**
B. **Situational**
C. **Visionary**
D. **Transactional**
E. **Value Based**
F. **Intuitive**
G. **Hierarchical**

My preferred style/s _____

My back up style/s _____

The styles explained

As a leader it is important to recognize where your strengths lie, where your blind sides are and which styles you feel most comfortable using. Most of you will have a preference for one style; however, you will probably also use some of the other styles on occasions. Each of the seven approaches to leadership has benefits and down sides. No one style is the correct style rather it is important to be aware of your preference and the range of styles you use. The analysis from the questionnaire and the information that follows should raise your awareness and also help you to think about areas for development to help you become a more authentic and versatile leader.

Different leadership styles: Key qualities

Benefits	Downsides
Participative – people using this style value the involvement of others above all else. Participative leaders actively seek people's opinions, thoughts and ideas. If you use this style effectively you will undoubtedly have excellent communication skills and be regarded as someone who collaborates and seeks consensus when leading, influencing and working with others.	On the downside some people may regard you as someone who doesn't know their own mind and takes too long to make decisions. Additionally, you may be regarded as someone who worries too much about involving and collaborating with others all the time.
Situational – if you use this style your tendency will be to analyze and evaluate the situation and then select what you believe to be the best approach to suit the prevailing circumstances. If used effectively you will be regarded as someone who is flexible, adaptable and capable.	If used ineffectively then you may be regarded as someone who is unpredictable and chameleon like. People like consistency so it is important for those who use this style to make sure that colleagues they are leading know them well enough to understand their behavior varies in order to get the best out of situations and people.
Visionary – this style relies to a large extent upon personal qualities – charisma, confidence and creativity are probably the most important. Visionaries are inspirational and use energy and enthusiasm to gain commitment to action. They are usually people who are articulate, confident communicators and capable of getting buy in to ideas through emotional appeal. They are often regarded as people who can paint pictures with words in order to engage with others.	The negative aspect of this style is mainly in the areas of structure, objectivity and data. Visionaries can overly rely on their enthusiasm and excitement about an issue and forget that some people like data, logic and structure to back up the vision. You may also be regarded as impractical and illogical.
Transactional – these leaders issue orders and directions and expect them to be met. They work on the basis that people know the structures, rules, rewards and punishments and pay little regard to the emotional element of their relationships. They expect others to follow their lead. It is very much a telling style, and while not universally popular in today's contemporary business world, it is a style that is useful in some situations – for instance	Overuse of this style has significant downsides not least of which is that it can be demotivating and can come across as disinterest in others – always expecting others to do it your way. This can have the effect of the leader being in a very lonely place when things go wrong and no one offers support.

(Continued)

Benefits	Downsides
when you are under time pressure, when safety or security are at risk and possibly when you know there is only one direction to follow. Often people who rely on this style are experts in an area and become used to others asking for their professional advice. However, giving expert advice is different from leadership. When leading you are not only giving advice but also developing relationships where inevitably emotions are involved.	
Value Based – people who use this style are usually highly principled and hold strong personal values which are used as a guide to much of how they live their lives. This style's success relies to a large extent on working with like-minded people towards a common goal. Followers of value-based leaders will know exactly what the leader stands for and will align with them.	The main disadvantage with this style is when people don't buy in to your ideals. Sometimes being value based can be a double-edged sword and sticking to one's principles means there's little room for flexibility. Lack of the consideration of a wider range of options can lead to being regarded as stubborn, obdurate or arrogant.
Intuitive – this style relies on a person's instinct where they use their innate qualities and capabilities to lead others. Intuitive leaders are confident in their own ability and demonstrate self belief based on their experience of previous success. Typically a leader who uses this style has learned much through the different experiences they have had in life. They use whole life experiences to inform their approach.	Intuitive leaders rely on their gut feel and while this is commendable in many situations sometimes it is not appropriate especially when an expert or particular course of action is required. Intuitive leaders may also find it difficult to justify and give reasons for their decisions or actions and are often heard to say *'it's just a feeling'*!
Hierarchical – this type of leadership is based on authority and level in the organization. A person's status is important here, if you are senior to another person then you are the leader – there is no reference at all to what one knows only the position you hold.	Sometimes it is necessary for the most senior person to take the lead and make a decision but if overly relied upon this style can become counterproductive as it is based on the premise that 'I'm the boss do as you are told.'

No one style can be regarded as best. Each of them has merits and downsides and certainly in today's complex business environment often a blend of styles is required. Even when using the most popular styles you can overly rely on one approach and end up failing to achieve your goals. The important thing to understand is where your particular preferences lie, how you deploy your skills and abilities to use that style and whether it is a successful style for you. You also need to be aware of timing and when you have to move from one style to another. In order to understand success you will need feedback from others. There is no easy way of getting this – you have to ask for it, listen to it and be willing to act on it (for ideas about feedback see later Chapter 9 on Career Planning).

Many of the women in our study identified situations where they had varied their style. This illustrates the point that for many of you adaptability is a feature of your leadership approach. For instance,

> I am now better at approaching people in different ways – adapting my style according to the person who is sitting opposite to me and using different approaches including a tougher approach when required. I was aware that my natural style works well with some people but not with others and my coach has really helped in providing the theory and experience in this area.

> I would describe myself as a collaborative leader and my team tells me that I have a good, open door policy. They feel that they can come and talk to me about anything and it's minimal hierarchy. However, I do balance being collaborative alongside being clear and directive; giving guidelines and deadlines – otherwise people lack the direction they need.
>
> **Interview quotes**

Guimei Pan describes women's leadership in China. 'Male leaders can be more directive in China, and this is seen by their employees as decisiveness, but generally women are admired if they have a more gentle coaching style. People do not feel comfortable with a woman manager who is too aggressive in her style – they would say she is not a woman, and it would go against them in most companies.' Guimei Pan went on to tell us that she has evolved her own style of decisiveness that in a European company might be described as tough love.

About a quarter of the women in our study felt that the prevailing leadership approach in their organization had had an impact upon the way they led others. Many of these women did not see this as a bad thing. Some cited that being influenced by their organization's culture and developing a style to suit that culture had worked well. For instance, 'My style is consistent with our organisational values', 'It's a style that fits comfortably with my natural style so there is no tension' and 'I have chosen where I can operate my own approach. Or I have left'. In fact most women felt that when the organization had had an impact on their way of leading it had been a good thing as they had learned to adapt their style which is a useful skill to develop for senior leadership positions.

ORIENTATIONS FOR SUCCESS

As a leader in business today there are certain key skills and abilities that you have to develop. Typically these skills fall into a range of different categories – for instance, strategic skills, business skills, inter-personal skills and personal skills. The following framework is based on research with over 1000 senior managers which was undertaken by the Ashridge Psychometric Services Department and encompasses a typical range of skills and abilities that any leader should aim to develop. Use the framework that is presented in the box to quickly assess your own skill level and the level of importance to you in your current role. (See Chapter 9 for a more detailed exercise exploring leadership skills.)

A framework of leadership skills and abilities

87

Most business people begin to develop these skills day to day and on the job or possibly while attending leadership training. Successful leaders recognize the importance of developing these skills in order to be able to do their job to the best of their ability. What is less clear is where women should focus their attention to ensure they make best use of their talents and position themselves for career development and promotion.

In many recent research studies which focus on women in business, women on boards and women leaders, there are two themes which constantly occur – networking and confidence. Taking this information together with the various conversations we have had, we have developed the following model to represent the four key areas on which women should focus in addition to the key competences that are mentioned above. These factors, we believe, are key areas that make a difference:

Career Success Factor Model

Relationship

Personal

Orientations
for success

Development

Achievement

Relationship orientation

Many of the women we surveyed said that they simply didn't have the right connections. This was expressed in many different ways, including comments about the *'old boys' network being alive and well'*, *'no senior female role models'*, *'male dominated environments'*, *'not having time to network'* and *'lack of inclination to network as hard work will pay off in the end'*. On the other hand we also heard stories of women who realized the importance of networking as a vital skill. In some ways the word networking does not give sufficient weight to what we mean here. Networking is a good starting point but there is so much more to it. Dame Sally Davies sees this as *'building friendships and alliances'*, which is much more than networking; *'it's a deeper relationship with someone who I respect and where usually we have shared values and interests.'*

In our experience it's not so much that women are not networked and connected; it's more about having the right connections and leveraging these connections. Generally women are less likely to use their networks to help them in their career, believing that their skills, abilities and achievements speak for themselves.

Adopting more of a relationship orientation and actively developing this throughout your career will ensure that you keep in touch with people. Recognize how and when people can help you, planning which networks you need and want to identify with. Internal organizational networks are of course of real benefit but then so are external networks. This tends to be the weaker area for many women. However, several of the women we interviewed also talked about their external connections. One talked about the importance of joining professional associations, Gill Collinson recognized the benefit of her early exposure to committee work and conference presentation and Dame Sally Davies highlighted relationships with people who are experts in their field. What they have all realized is that good quality relationships and connections help enormously in reputation development.

Being more tuned into and developing a willingness and capability to network will pay dividends. An additional benefit of being well connected throughout your career relates to reputation and credibility. Your network will often prove to be your best supporters and references. So much business at senior levels is done through word of mouth and personal recommendation. Making sure that you are connected to the right people will mean that you will have a network of friends and colleagues willing to recommend you.

Personal orientation

Lack of confidence and self belief both play a role in holding women back. We explored this in Chapter 5. So, what can you do to develop and demonstrate self belief and confidence? Aspects of both self belief and confidence undoubtedly relate to your overall personality and we know this is something you cannot change. What you can do is change behavior to develop skills, approaches and attitudes that will contribute to a feeling of greater self belief and confidence.

Here are some simple things you can do on your own:

- Make a list of all your achievements so far – it is important to be specific here. Go back through the whole of your life, start at school, college and early jobs right up to today; think about family achievements, hobbies and interests as well as your career. Once you've made this list you should celebrate your success so far. Actually listing and seeing what you've accomplished in your life can give you quite a boost in self confidence as well as helping you to understand your strengths. (See also Chapter 9 – Timeline exercise.)
- Focus on those things that you do well. Record what it is you do, how you do it, when you do it and what the outcomes are. Once you understand more about your strengths and how you deploy them successfully you can then plan how to demonstrate these characteristics more frequently in your day-to-day life. Focusing, building on and developing your strengths will contribute to increased feelings of confidence and self belief.
- It is also worth listing those things you feel disappointed about not achieving. Once you've listed the disappointments spend some time reflecting about what it was that stopped you achieving these targets. Understanding what stops you achieving will help you to recognize similar situations and conditions in the future and to plan ahead to avoid similar disappointments. In addition to this, once you've identified these blockers it will be worth working with a coach or mentor to develop coping strategies which should also help you to be more self confident.
- Understand how you deal with failure. Failing at something can, at best, be a nuisance that gets in your way for a while but you get over it and move on. On the other hand, it can be something that damages your confidence and challenges your credibility. We all deal with failure in different ways; the important thing is to understand how you deal with it and how resilient you are in bouncing back.
- Know your weaknesses. It is of real benefit to know those things that you are not good at, skills and abilities that require development. By acknowledging these areas of weakness you can plan how best to develop them.

Achievement orientation

This is about knowing what you want to achieve, understanding your ambitions and being willing to express them appropriately. Many of the people who responded to our questionnaire indicated that they felt that they had been hindered in their career because:

- They were unwilling to express their ambitions, seeing this as aggressive or boasting.
- They didn't want to put themselves forward for an opportunity because they did not fit the profile exactly.
- They suffered from imposter syndrome because they felt they might be found out as incapable or lacking in qualifications.
- They knew that someone else had been earmarked for the role (often a man) and they didn't think it was worth applying.
- They didn't think they were ready for the role yet.
- They waited for someone (usually a boss) to recognize their talents and skills and then promote them based on merit.

Many women also indicated that early in their career they had been less ambitious or less aware of the importance of demonstrating an achievement orientation as they wanted to focus on the job in hand and get to grips with this before thinking about the next stage. Of course you also have to understand what we as women mean by ambition and for many of us this isn't simply about getting to the top or climbing the corporate ladder; it also seems to be about working with interesting people, working in an environment that matches your values, doing work that is worthwhile, building your skill and competence base and being valued for what you do by your organization, boss and colleagues. Climbing the corporate ladder, getting promotion and being appropriately rewarded are all in there; it's just that you often have other considerations to think about as well.

Having a plan for your career, knowing what you want to achieve and constantly refreshing this plan is a good starting point. It is also worth remembering that having a plan is good, but sticking rigidly to this can be bad – plans change, ideas develop and new opportunities present themselves at the strangest times and in the strangest ways. Having a plan means that you can adapt and adjust your plan from a position of knowledge, strength and awareness rather than just wandering through your career or moving to the next job because it is there or the timing is right.

Some of the women we interviewed talked about taking on new roles simply as a stepping stone to something better knowing that the role was about skill development and positioning rather than their dream job. Most of these women realized the importance of demonstrating achievement orientation early on in their career.

Development orientation

Taking responsibility for your own development and recognizing early on in your career that it is your, and only your, responsibility is important. Develop antennae to recognize and take advantage of development opportunities as they arise. Being achievement oriented and having a career plan will help you to create and select the most appropriate development opportunities as they present themselves.

The key to good development orientation is to be aware of the rich variety of opportunities available to you. These opportunities can fall into two broad categories:

- **Formal development** – planned opportunities, including training courses, further education programs, seminars, workshops and coaching.
- **Informal development** – workplace training including secondments, projects, special assignments, mentor relationships, self managed learning including web-based training, podcasts, webinars and online self study courses.

In order to be truly development oriented not only is it necessary to be aware of the various opportunities for development, but also to make sure that the development method is most appropriate for the skill being developed and also suits your own learning style. You may also find that it is best to use a variety of different methods to develop your skills. So, for instance, when developing change management skills you could start by attending a short formal training workshop to raise your awareness of a range of the approaches and techniques for success and to share ideas and practice skills in a safe environment. This could then be followed by taking on a special project which involves managing a change process in your organization where you can then try things out in real life getting feedback on your performance as you go along. In addition to this you may find that working with a coach helps you to reflect and further develop your skills. Perhaps the most important element of development orientation is to make use of as many different methods as possible.

SUMMARY

The complex area of leadership is one that can rarely be completely mastered. All you can hope to do is to understand your own style, skills and approaches and know what you can do to develop these further in order to be even more effective. As we have seen from our research, as well as from other studies, women have fewer role models than men and often find it challenging to compete on equal terms with their male colleagues for career success. Additionally in our work at Ashridge we see some business people who hold leadership positions for years before clearly understanding their style, strengths and strategies. So, our tips are:

1. **Develop your leadership strategy** – Know your skills, abilities and play to your strengths
2. **Being tougher than the men!** From our research, and our teaching and consultancy experience, we know of some organizations where senior women have felt it necessary to adopt existing male/macho leadership styles; their aim is to be as tough, if not tougher, than the men. We do think that it's possible to take a different approach and perhaps the younger generation of women leaders will feel confident enough to do this. We also would offer some advice – macho leadership should not be seen as an 'ideal', as it often creates a toxic culture of fear that is not healthy for the organization
3. **Vision** – Be clear about your personal leadership vision
4. **Understand your preferred leadership style/s** – and develop the skill to flex this when necessary. Be honest with yourself about your preferences, any limitations and work with others to get feedback
5. **Be authentic** – Be true to yourself and feel comfortable with your leadership style
6. **Explore your leadership image with others** – Ask for feedback about your style and impact and the impression you create. Examples from the political arena where women have recognized the need to manage their image for greater success are:
   - Margaret Thatcher used voice coaching to create a deeper sound to improve her performance when speaking in the crowded and noisy House of Commons chamber.
   - Gro Harlem Brundtland, who was three times Prime Minister of Norway, when asked about her advice for young women politicians highlights the voice – '... *one thing I'm sure about is that if you have a high-pitched voice, like many women have, that becomes*

(Continued)

thin and not easy to hear. You have to speak up. So I usually tell women: You must train your voice and you must use it by being heard. Because you are not going to be respected fully if people don't sense that you speak with a certain authority.'[1] The same is true for young businesswomen.

7

THE ORGANIZATIONAL LANDSCAPE

I think men are judged to be more experienced than women of the same age and background.

In my organisation there's a closer watch on women managers – there are so few of us.

Survey quotes

These comments illustrate that organizational life continues to be a less than level playing field for women in the 21st century, and are typical of what was said by many women involved in our research. We also heard more positive views from women, as one director at a large software company said,

I've been lucky as I've never experienced discrimination in my career.

Survey quote

The problem is that this more positive environment does not exist everywhere. In many respects things have improved, not least the increasing number of women graduates in recent years. However, some issues remain stubbornly resistant to change. In the early 1960s President Kennedy set up a commission to investigate the status of women in America and asked Eleanor Roosevelt to lead it. (The commission was in return for her support for John F Kennedy's presidential campaign.) These events may seem a long time ago so it's interesting (if somewhat depressing) to note that the findings are still relevant today. One example is about pay inequality.

Pay inequality is one of the European Union's current campaigns – a response to a continuing gender pay gap which on average is 17.5 percent. This gap has hardly altered for over a decade now and in some countries – such as the UK, Austria and also Germany – it's higher, at around 20 percent.[1] Why? Well we know that part-time work patterns are not the only explanation, as equal pay audits and research identify differences between men and women recruited at the same time, who are working at the same level, are equally well qualified, etc. One woman said,

> *At a European meeting recently the leadership team for the project put up a slide to show some details about themselves – and included how much they were paid. This showed that the only woman on the team of 15 earns far, far less than all the others!*
>
> **Survey quote**

Another worrying trend which connects the 1960s commission with today is the scarcity of women at senior and board levels.

> *Among the 40 or so managers involved in our executive team, there are only two women – myself and another woman.*
>
> *The senior team in my organisation has ten men and one woman – the HR director.*
>
> **Survey quotes**

The appointment of a female chief executive can serve as a great role model for other women in the organization. Jill McDonald was appointed chief executive for McDonald's UK at the end of 2010 (the surname is coincidental as there is no family connection). She was surprised at the number of messages and emails[2] sent by female staff who were delighted to see her promoted from her marketing role to become the first woman CEO in the UK company.

There is also a continuing view that women managers are acceptable, but only in some roles:

> *There is a glass ceiling perception regarding women in brewing unless you are in HR, marketing or communications.*
>
> **Survey quote**

We heard similar remarks about other sectors, such as financial services, the oil industry and about countries such as Germany and Switzerland.

I am in a male dominated, German based organisation and I am the only female head of division. The German culture is very male orientated.
Survey quote

This limited pool of women leaders creates a number of problems, not least about how women behave in terms of communication, leadership style and the absence of role models. A 2011 study of financial services[3] mentions the absence of female sponsors and the impact of this. Baroness Sarah Hogg, a well-known and respected director of several FTSE 100 companies, has described how she felt in the 1990s when she first entered a boardroom. The established styles she found then were either a 'helpless little woman' or 'headmistress'.[4] Things have moved on from such extreme stereotypes but while so few blue-chip employers have women at board level, questions of communication, leadership style and role models remain important issues. Research by Dr Judith Baxter among board level directors in seven UK firms found that women tended to choose more apologetic and self-deprecating language while the men studied were more direct and confrontational.[5]

The following table illustrates some key changes that have happened over the years:

What's changed for working women: Comparing the 20th and the 21st century

Time Period	The 20th century – in particular the 1960s/70s and 80s	The 21st century
Career ambitions	Many women graduates aspire to be teachers. Few enter business to take management roles	Far more equality in terms of ambition though still a clear tendency for women to take HR, PR and marketing roles. Progress is happening at a different pace in some countries e.g., in the Middle East
Pay	Considerable inequality with regard to pay	Salaries are fairer and most organizations (and the legislation) accept the principle that 'men and women should be rewarded equally for work of equal value' – though at senior level this still remains a problem

(Continued)

Lifestyle	Women at senior corporate levels are usually single and those who were married did not have children. A number of organizations (and sectors such as teaching) had a policy for women to retire upon marriage. The Foreign Office lifted its marriage bar in 1972	There are more working mothers at senior levels but it's still tough to combine/balance family with key senior/operational roles
Numbers	It is unusual to see women managers – most women in business meetings were assumed to be secretaries	The number of women managers has increased but few at senior levels – fewer still at board level. Most blue-chip organizations (around 9 out of 10) have yet to appoint a woman at board level (either as an executive or as non-executive)
Language and attitudes	Most women working at this lime can tell shocking stories about sexist attitudes. This is highlighted by the 1980 Hollywood comedy film *Nine to Five* starring Dolly Parton and Jane Fonda where three women work for, and out-wit, their chauvinistic boss	We talk these days about 'being p.c. or 'being politically correct' – which means that earlier sexist remarks and behavior are no longer acceptable in the workplace. They are also illegal and a company might be sued for discrimination

© Dent and Holton, 2012.
Note: A timeline of women's achievements appears in Appendix A.

We asked the women involved in our research to describe critical incidents which have helped shape their careers. As might be expected some of these concern personal events such as children, divorce, death and illness. Children are undoubtedly a blessing as well as presenting a career problem for many. Their comments also identify what (or who) helped them within the organization and the rest of this chapter focuses on these topics. We then consider what organizations and HR can learn from this.

CRITICAL CAREER INCIDENTS

The critical incidents identified by women did include some stories about overt discrimination as shown in the following quote and others highlight difficulties caused by working for someone with poor management skills:

> *I was not given a promotion to senior vice-president HR in my previous company as I was pregnant with my second child. The fact that I returned to work after six weeks did not make a difference!*
>
> **Survey quote**

We found four broad themes described as critical incidents, namely,

1. Mentors, sponsors, coaches and line managers as key supporters;
2. Opportunities that arise from taking on significant projects or promotions;
3. The challenge of combining children with a career;
4. The importance of building resilience.

Each of these is briefly described in the sections below.

THE ROLE OF KEY SUPPORTERS

The first theme is about the role of key supporters and how they can assist individuals. Many survey respondents and every woman leader we interviewed talk about the role taken by supporters and mentors. Sponsors, people in the organization who help promote the individual to others, are also mentioned. Women's networks and alumni groups within the business can also make a difference.

Sometimes, as one woman explained it was *'having a brilliant mentor from the start'* and often this is the boss, the supervisor or the line manager. Many describe how important it has been to have someone who can see their capability and can help them develop key skills and experiences that they need to move their career to a more senior level:

> *I have worked for at least three very supportive bosses, usually at CEO level who have given me opportunities to develop.*
>
> **Survey quote**

Advice from a coach has also played a part in defining what individuals want in their career, as shown in the illustration that follows.

Illustration: The importance of a good career coach

Birgitte Ladefoged is HR Senior Director at Danfoss A/S. Looking back on her career, one critical incident she describes came from a coaching intervention which helped her think through and really appreciate her career 'values'. The skills of the coach really focused her and helped her re-evaluate what was most important to her. It was invaluable in helping her plan her next career move:

> I have two kids and when they were quite young I worked at home as a consultant in my own company for about 18 months. Then I went to see a coach because I thought it was best for me to have my own company, to work when I liked to work, and to stay with my family and my kids when I wanted that and so on.
>
> But I had this very good coach who made me see that the most important part for me actually in my job position is to be a part of something bigger. The dialogue with my coach was a real turning point for me actually, because I saw much more clearly that I needed employees around me and a team to work with. I also liked the leadership part, I enjoy being a leader, and so the coaching sessions were revealing for me.

The power and impact of coaching is clear but you have to be open-minded to take such feedback. Clive Woodward is admired as an outstanding sports coach and his comment about great sports performers could in our view just as easily be said about great business leaders:

> I've never met a quality player intent on winning who didn't want to hear about ways they could improve his or her game.

OPPORTUNITIES AND THE CHANCE TO TAKE ON BIG PROJECTS

The second theme regards the scale of opportunities, the chance to take on challenging roles and a number of individuals describe major projects or promotions among their critical incidents:

> I was working with Booz Allen Hamilton on a £50m fixed cost reduction project (30 per cent of fixed costs) in the first two years of my career which directly reported to the organisational board.

> One major restructure allowed me to put myself forward for a more senior role than perhaps I would have otherwise been considered for. This promotion has enabled me to develop my career to Head of HR.

Moving to London to take up the role of head of internal audit with no internal audit experience – high risk but high reward. The job worked out and gave me a much higher profile which led to other jobs.

I did a two month secondment to our Paris office. As well as the opportunity to work in another office, I was also able to cover a role at the level above mine so it gave me a real opportunity for growth and to prove that I was capable.

I have had fantastic training and development opportunities with Avon where I worked for six years both in the UK and in other countries.

Survey quotes

Most examples we heard about were tailor-made, designed for the individual in question. However, organizations could do more to provide such opportunities for groups of staff, e.g., the opportunity to join a central pool of interim managers for short, say three or six month, stints. Small action groups led by senior staff would be another way that a wider group could gain such experience or the example noted above – the chance to cover for a role at a more senior level.

Finally, a word of warning for any organization which has scaled down (in terms of people and/or resources) – it's really important to provide sufficient space and flexibility so individuals can seek out, and learn from, development opportunities. Providing such opportunities for individuals will help them to become better managers so it also means that the quality of the management team overall will likewise improve.

THE CHALLENGE OF COMBINING CAREERS AND CHILDREN

The challenge, perhaps conflict is a better word, of combining a career with having children is another theme in the critical incidents. There was a time, a few years ago, when many women senior managers were either single or married without children. That is changing; these days there's a younger generation who want to have a good career and manage to bring up children – but it is tough. As one participant explained,

Having to work long and inflexible hours and travel abroad to the US – being bent out of shape while have two kids under three and trying to work as if I didn't have any children.

Survey quote

One problem highlighted in our research is the gap that sometimes develops between what organizations say and what they actually do i.e., *'we treat everyone equally'*. Others appear to cling to old-fashioned work practices:

> *My organisation is really progressive when it comes to helping working mothers. But I hear often about others that are back in the Dark Ages and have almost Dickensian [19th century/old-fashioned] attitudes, when it comes to helping working parents. They have a totally inflexible approach to flexible working.*

Survey quote

Some readers may respond to these issues saying that OK, yes it's tough for women who want careers and families but it also affects many men. We would agree and say that improvements, and a more family-friendly workplace, will help both men and women.

Illustration: Work–life balance

Dame Sally Davies acknowledges in a classic English under-statement that her work–life balance is not so good at the moment. Dealing with not one but two demanding jobs at the top of the Civil Service (during the early part of 2011) means that in addition to a tough work load there are engagements three or four evenings a week. She does say however, that this current phase is temporary and the future will settle back to something more manageable.

Many years ago she was told by a neighbor how many people on good salaries often economized on the wrong things, namely childcare and looking after the family – *'it was an observation that I internalised and we've never penny pinched on childcare. Over the years the family was extremely fortunate to find and keep a wonderful live-in nanny who was with us for 16 years from the beginning when one of the children was born. We fell over backwards to treat her well and with respect right from the start. While she was with us she got "A" levels and a B.Ed. degree. She did well out of it and we did too.'*

The children of the family, who are now 19 and 16 years old, think that she got it all about right over the years – *'I asked them a few days ago whether it would have been better with me full-time and the answer was a definite no!'*

Has it got any easier these days for working mothers? No, she says, it's still a problem especially for those with younger children. *'You do feel guilty*

(Continued)

and that is inevitable.' With regard to holidays, Dame Sally takes all her holiday allowance and says it is important to her to have this time with the family. There is a trend in some parts of the public (and also the private sector) not to take all holiday entitlement, almost a statement of the importance of the job or the individual. Though sometimes this also stems from feeling vulnerable – a worry about job security. Whatever the reason it is a contributory factor in the growing problem of stress and burn-out which is evident in many organizations these days.

THE IMPORTANCE OF BUILDING RESILIENCE

Resilience is a key quality for successful leaders and is the fourth theme or critical incident identified in our research. Resilience often includes high-energy, positive thinking and motivation, for example, someone who is different to those around them and can enjoy re-framing issues and sees set-backs as challenges. It doesn't mean someone who is mistakenly optimistic all the time; it's about the ability to bounce back, and to re-frame negative issues into learning opportunities.

Sometimes personal illness illustrates this quality in people and we noticed that some respondents describe seemingly negative experiences becoming transformational.

An Ashridge colleague – Alex Davda – has developed a resilience questionnaire that may be of value to both individuals and organizations. See URL link below for more information and to assess your own qualities. www.ashridge.org.uk/resilience

A CORPORATE STRATEGY: WHAT ORGANIZATIONS NEED TO FOCUS ON

Individual change is important, for example individuals taking ownership for their own career destiny, but organizations also need to change. It's important to have a structured, business-led, approach to help create a good environment for women at all levels of the business. It's important to have curiosity rather than complacency – a curious company will be actively looking for ways to improve. A complacent company will rely more upon its published statement of equality which may, or may not, accurately reflect what is happening for women who work there.

Richard Feynman's name is well known in physics and his influence has been compared to Einstein. He was an eccentric who was immensely funny, gave great lectures and liked to play the bongo drums when he wasn't being a physicist. These facts are perhaps intriguing and may possibly inspire readers to find out more about him (see YouTube). However, his relevance to this book is for his approach to learning and knowledge. He spent his whole life being curious and as a result created nanotechnology (among many other achievements). An organization that is curious with a genuine interest in developing new ideas will help women reach their full potential. Accenture is a good example of this as shown in the following illustration:

Illustration: Accenture's support for women:

- Women's mentoring programs pair female executives with senior executive mentors. This includes virtual workshops and provides networking tips to help ensure the advancement of women.
- Accenture Women's Network is a global internal website that connects women across the company with one another and provides access to resources available in-house and externally. The online forum offers women a place to share experiences, advice and insights.

The program is supported and championed at senior level. Such support is important for any change program and it also makes the difference for any initiatives aimed at helping women managers. Training for diversity awareness as well as courses directed toward developing women leaders are available. In the Developing High-Performing Women course, female role models help managers evaluate requirements to reach the next stage in their careers. To date, more than 550 women from 23 countries have participated in the program.

Source: With permission from Accenture. Edited from website (www.accenture.com/us-en/company/people/women/Pages/womens-programs-initiatives.aspx), accessed March 2011.

Johnson & Johnson also has a Women's Leadership Initiative which began in the 1990s and this has helped increase the number of women at executive committee and senior line appointments.

A LEADERSHIP ROLE FOR HR?

Human Resources do not always get a good press with regard to creating change or reviewing how policies and procedures can help women leaders. It often does better at compliance, ensuring that legislation (at national and international level) is met. HR could do much more. This generally, although not always, requires business leadership – an enlightened chief executive and/or a senior executive team who can see the moral and business value of change. There seem to be three different approaches in how HR deals with diversity issues:

A leadership role for HR?

Level 1
HR diversity leaders

Level 2
HR limited interest

Level 3
HR diversity
compliant

Level 1. HR diversity leaders – an example here is McDonald's, winners of HR Magazine's 2010 Award 'HR Excellence Award – Best Workplace Diversity Strategy'. The judges praised the way that diversity policies are brought alive – *'not just something that exists in company handbooks'*. It's an important distinction in ensuring change occurs in the organization. (Santander and Tesco were among the finalists for the award.)

Level 2. HR limited interest – a term which applies to organizations where the HR team (and recruitment advertising) may describe some of the principles of diversity e.g., *'everyone is encouraged to develop their full potential'* but in reality little or no effort is applied to identifying the barriers which hold women managers back. There are many organizations which are at this level (and level 3 above); a 2011 survey found that of 1,800 HR professionals polled, 71 percent said their organization did not have a clearly defined strategy or philosophy for developing women for leadership roles.[6]

Level 3. HR diversity compliant – this describes an organization where the legal minimum is thought sufficient; *we are doing
what's required in order to avoid being sued for discrimination'*. Or, as
mentioned above, does it rely on an equality statement as evidence
that all is well? www.humanresourcesmagazine.com/news/1012576/
HR-Excellence-Awards-2010-Best-Workplace-Diversity-Strategy---
Winner-McDonalds/ accessed March 2011

Another award, voted for by readers of 'Woman Engineer' magazine
in 2011, placed Lockheed Martin, Siemens and General Electric at the
top of a survey of 'Top 50 Employers'. www.eop.com/awards-EO.php
accessed March 2011.

A simple way to create more change is to ask, *'What more could we
do to help women leaders?'* instead of the more common and conservative HR question, *'Will we pass the legal requirements test on equality?'*
Bureaucratic rules and regulations often hold back change with regard
to flexible working and often there is a culture where the emphasis is
about 'what's not permitted'.

Illustration: The role of women at senior levels

*I think we are not even close yet in my organisation to what would be OK for
women. I think it's around eight per cent of the top managers are women
and when we look at the five divisions there are around 45 top managers
together with our Executive Committee there are two women in this group
including me. It's definitely not enough. I'm an HR person and so people
say, 'well, HR is always women'. The other woman on this level is our R&D
Vice President, so this is quite interesting because she's the first woman to
influence our development and our future products.*

Survey quote

EXERCISE

Key questions for organizations:

- How would you describe the HR approach to diversity? What's the
  key question used – is it the minimum of *'are we doing enough to
  avoid being accused of discrimination?'* A far better question is *'what
  more could we do to help women?'*
- How often do you ask women in your organization about the challenges they face and what support would help them?

- How much support is available for women leaders? Are women equally likely as men to win promotion at senior level?
- How often does the board discuss gender and equality issues? Is there senior level and CEO commitment for initiatives designed to help women?

A key strategy which we believe would help increase the number of women leaders in future years, is the notion of a Leadership Academy (for both men and women) as part of an organization's talent management process. The model shown in the figure that follows summarizes our thinking in this area and suggests what a Leadership Academy needs to include:

Six circles of a leadership academy

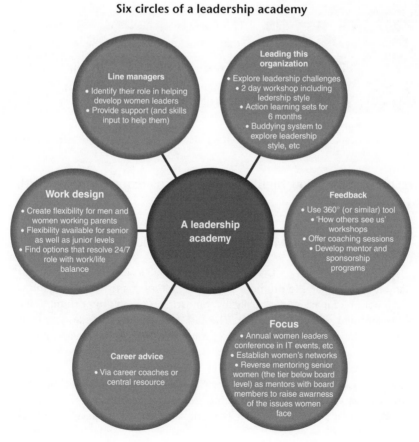

© Holton 2012

This of course would apply to the whole workforce and therefore some readers (and diversity experts) may disagree with our advice and say instead that a specific diversity plan, rather than a leadership academy, is more important. However, some diversity plans do not include a focus on helping women leaders or on ensuring that the younger generation of women can thrive and are equally likely as men to get those tough tasks and opportunities which make all the difference when it comes to promotion. We would also argue that what's planned for should be measured – the following table is a good benchmark as it includes data about promotion at senior level.

Accenture's metrics

Women in the workforce	35 per cent of the workforce are women (among 70,000 people.)
	In 2010 34 per cent of new hires were women.
Women leaders	More than 16 per cent of senior executives and 25 per cent of the global management committee are women. There also are 3 women on the Board.
	Women represent 20 per cent of promotions to senior executive level.

From company website, with permission.

Source: www.accenture.com/us-en/company/people/diversity/Pages/index.aspx, accessed March 2011.

The illustration below highlights how much change can occur within a few years.

Illustration – IBM's approach to diversity, 1995 to 1999

The Executive Women's Diversity Task Force began in July 1995, with an ambitious mandate: to promote significant culture change in the organization both nationally and globally, by improving women's opportunities for development and advancement. The task force began by asking women leaders about their perceptions regarding the barriers to advancement. A formal, six-month examination of these issues resulted in the creation of numerous sub-committees with an emphasis on global concerns. The various task forces – the Women of Colour and Women in Technology, the Global Women Leaders' Steering Committee and programs such as Mentoring and Employee Development – empowered, developed and advanced diverse individuals throughout IBM. Specific global-focused components included a work/life survey in Latin America; a work/life survey in Europe, the largest work/life survey in the world; Global Women's Leadership conferences; a global dependent care assessment; the institution of global women's networks and women's council; and a global partnership promoting flexibility in the workplace.

As a champion of IBM's Task Force initiative, CEO and Chairman, Lou Gerstner encouraged a *'top–down, bottom–up'* approach to culture change. He communicated personal commitment to employees through letters, e-mails and postings on the company's Intranet. Managers were required to attend diversity training courses, conduct departmental diversity meetings and promote attendance at diversity town hall gatherings. At the same time, constituency groups were encouraged to drive the culture change and diversity agenda by identifying their needs and opportunities for change. Accountability at IBM is strong: managers are accountable for meeting diversity results; Gerstner in turn reported results directly to IBM's Board of Directors. Evaluations for both executives and managers included sections on commitment to diversity efforts.

Women's representation at the executive level worldwide increased steadily since the start of the initiative, Global Women Leaders' Task Force: Creating the Climate to Win:

North America	1995	women comprised 14 per cent of all executives
	1999	21 per cent
Asia-Pacific	1995	women executive representation was 1 per cent
	1999	8 per cent
Latin America	1995	no women executives
	1999	5 per cent of executives
Europe, Middle	1995	women executive representation was 2 per cent
East and Africa	1999	8 per cent

In fact, in total since year end 1995, the number of women in executive level positions has increased 175 per cent and now totals over 500 women executives around the world.

Source: Taken from Catalyst website of 2000 award winners and edited – with permission from Catalyst and IBM.

www.catalyst.org/publication/118/ibm-corporationglobal-women-leaders-task-force-creating-the-climate-to-win accessed March 2011.

WHAT ARE THE CURRENT ISSUES FOR ORGANIZATIONS?

What do organizations need to do in order to create a better environment for women? In our view there are a few key pieces of advice. The first of these is the potential danger in the current discussions about the need to appoint more women at board level. It is possible that a focus on board-level appointments may happen at the expense of another important goal – getting more women to senior management level. This second issue is critical because it's this senior group which will in due time become members of boards. Marjorie Scardino,[7] who is one of the few women FTSE 100 chief executives, summed this up in comments she made in 2010: *we don't need more women in the boardroom. We need more women in the top ranks of companies.* There's also a certain irony in recruiting women at board level from external sources if women within the company in question receive little (or no support). Companies need to be sure they look at both issues. Some other practical pieces of advice are highlighted below.

Advice to organizations

Stereotypes still exist about different jobs – organizations could do more to advertise technical roles in a more open way that attracts women, e.g., involving women in the recruitment process and taking people from different disciplines:

> When I look back to the recruitment team that Morgan Stanley sent out for IT roles it included 2 women and 3 men and it wasn't just people from engineering backgrounds; some had business backgrounds, others came from economics, English graduates, etc., and so it felt very open. In fact I was the only person they recruited with a technical background; the others came from a variety of different disciplines.
>
> **Survey quote**

Think about other stereotypes in the business which hold women back and take steps to challenge and change these. An example mentioned in the interviews is about assumptions made about potential women candidates – *'the new appointment has a lot of travel requirements – she's got a young family and so won't want to do that.'* It's particularly important where women are the minority group, e.g., with regard to international assignments one

Continued

company has around 700 managers (from around 50 different nationalities) who work outside their own country and only 20 percent are women. In other companies the number is much lower.

Don't expect women leaders to behave like men

Some core capabilities between men and women are common to both (as with a Venn diagram) but I do believe there are exceptions outside of that, and organisations should be open to a broader set of leadership traits. For example women will generally be more collaborative while men will be more controlled in the way they deliver messages.

Interview quote

We agree with this view. There also is an issue here about whether collaborative, so called 'people-friendly', styles of leadership are equally valued or are they seen as being less effective?

As Dame Sally Davies said, *'I don't want to be treated any differently because I am a woman but I am not an honorary man.'*

Few organizations review leadership in the way that Danone has. In March 2009 (with an update in June 2010) Danone held a women's leadership event in Evian. It was the first time this had happened and in the 2009 session 80 women and men considered the theme of male and female leadership. As a result one workgroup was set up on careers, another looked at development tools to help self-confidence as well as providing mentoring, coaching, etc.

With permission, accessed June 2010 from
www.danone.com/en/careers/commitment-towards-employees.html

REFLECTIVE EXERCISE

Think about how well your organization is doing in terms of each of the points above – does it create a good environment for women? Are there areas that could be improved?

A time for change?

We have identified a number of tensions which exist in the organizational landscape for women such as the difficulty of managing a demanding senior role (say a key operational appointment) with long working hours and being a working mother. Equal access to executive development, coaching and promotion opportunities is also important. Our survey findings below show some of the challenges which still exist:

- 49% believe men and women are judged differently in their organization in relation to leadership style and behavior.
- 48% believe it is harder for women to succeed in their organization compared to male colleagues.
- 44% believe men and women are judged unequally with regard to promotion in their organization.

All organizations need to review and consider whether they provide a positive environment for women. Rajni Gupta is Director of Compliance and Corporate Governance who works for Intercontinental Hotels and says, *'in my 20 years of working I have always worked for companies that respect capabilities and don't judge people by gender.'* She also observes that this approach has to be set by the behaviors and attitudes from the top leaders in the business.

The aim of the Leadership Academy described earlier in this chapter is to provide excellent support, encouragement and a career development infrastructure. These are of course the same building blocks of any good talent management system. Commitment by the chief executive and the senior executive team to identify barriers, and find solutions, are also essential in order to create a positive work environment for women. A re-design of working contracts along with a real commitment to flexible working (not just lip service or PR-speak) at senior level would ease the conflict that many working parents experience.

How good organizations support women managers

Senior level/CEO commitment and innovative ideas. Partnering for success: there needs to be a good partnership between the organization and women.	Flexible working (a real commitment rather than lip service), and a structure which helps women trying to balance a career and a family.
A Leadership Academy (or something similar) as described earlier in this chapter.	A first class career development structure with plenty of support, opportunities, feedback, coaching and career signposts.

Finally, a question for any business, 'would you win a diversity award?' The European diversity awards sponsored by Google began in 2011 gives some background about what's expected; see www.europeandiversityawards.com and http://twitter.com/diversityaward. The Catalyst campaign in the US and Opportunity Now in the UK also both run annual award schemes; see www.catalyst.org and www.opportunitynow.org.uk

Exercise: Creating more equality in your organization

Consider the check-list and identify how many of the ideas have been applied in your organization? A simple guideline is that the more items you can tick the better.

IDEAS TO CREATE MORE EQUALITY	YES	NO	UNDER REVIEW
1. Mentoring and coaching programs			
2. Identify overt diversity targets – in the same way as targets are used for other business and HR issues			
3. Review access to leadership events, executive development and encourage more women to attend			
4. Create a network for women leaders			
5. Partnership with other organizations to offer mentoring, secondments, job shadowing and shadow board schemes			
6. Undertake career reviews – what are the barriers and what are the solutions – for women?			
7. Skills development and targeting skills (and key experiences) that women will need for senior executive and director level appointments			
8. Role models for women at the top of the organization			
9. Support for individuals taking on key senior and operational roles in the business			

Continued

IDEAS TO CREATE MORE EQUALITY	YES	NO	UNDER REVIEW
10. Develop online (and individual) career development support for women at all levels			
11. Demonstrate senior commitment for diversity issues e.g., a diversity champion at board level; mentoring or coaching schemes between senior executives and women			
12. Review networking (especially networking events at senior levels) – do these make women feel included?			
13. Are 'softer' leadership skills discussed as part of executive education programs? Are women observers involved in assessment/development centers/ succession planning?			
14. Are career breaks encouraged (or are they seen as career limiting?); are there a variety of flexitime options for returning to work? One woman we interviewed designed a new contract – with 10 weeks' holiday each year – to help her balance a senior partner role and family issues. (It's been a great success and is now used by many other women in the firm.) Another innovator is a senior director with an operational role who spreads a demanding five-day workload across seven days.			
15. Do HR policies and procedures help women? Are line managers encouraged – and supported by HR – to offer flexible working options?			
16. Are equality questions included in the annual employee survey? The questions used by Shell are shown in the box that follows.			

HOW WELL ARE WE DOING IN REGARD TO DIVERSITY?
FIVE KEY QUESTIONS ABOUT DIVERSITY

❖ Where I work we are treated with respect.
❖ I am free to speak my mind without fear of negative consequences.
❖ My organization has a working environment in which different views and perspectives are valued.
❖ My organization has a working environment that is free from harassment and discrimination.
❖ The decisions leaders in my organization make concerning employees are fair.

Source: Shell Diversity and Inclusion Annual Report, 2010.www-static. shell.com/static/environment_society/downloads/commitments_standards/diversity_inclusion_brochure_2010.pdf accessed July 2011, with permission.

SUMMARY

Organizations have real opportunities to create more positive environments for women in business. The key areas for focus are:

1. **Ask women what help they want** – don't make assumptions
2. **Provide opportunities for new ways of working** – find out what the best organizations are doing in this area
3. **Be aware of diversity issues** – and ways to measure success and achievements
4. **Appoint a diversity champion at a senior level** – make it a board level issue
5. **Consider how proactive HR is with regard to diversity issues** – it needs to be more than simply adhering to the compliance issues
6. **Identify the key issues for promotion (especially to senior levels)** – make sure that women have equal access to the assignments and experiences that will make a difference to their CV.

8

CAREER ADVICE AND WHAT I WISH I'D KNOWN EARLIER IN MY CAREER

Make sure you have a good team, make sure you surround yourself with people you can trust – **Gillian Hibberd**

When an opportunity is offered, take it. Rather than thinking about five reasons why you can't do something think about why you can; take opportunities and take controlled risks

Survey quote

There are plenty of books that highlight *'how to plan your career'* but it is not as simple as some of these might suggest. Our research indicates that as many of us know from experience, there are lots of different factors and triggers which affect an individual career, not least the need to seize opportunities that are presented. There is definitely some truth in the phrase about *'being in the right place at the right time'*. Equally valuable is the ability that not all of us possess – being able to learn from mistakes and to move on quickly rather than dwelling on injustices or missed opportunities.

There are four key areas of career advice or themes which we have distilled from the survey and interview findings – as illustrated in the figure that follows. We asked women what advice they would give to others and also what did they wish they had known earlier in their own career. Most of the comments in the survey were about personal skill development, for example about confidence. But career processes and planning, relationships such as support from colleagues and organizational issues, as illustrated, were also highlighted.

Four key pieces of career advice for women

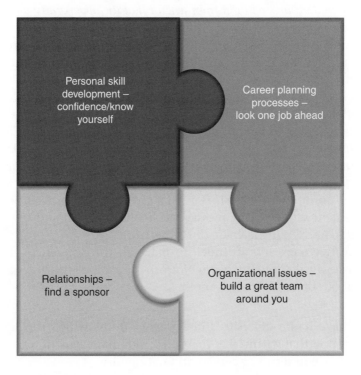

Each of these is discussed later in this chapter. Some of the four themes apply regardless of the size of the company; others such as the need to find a sponsor are more relevant if you work in a larger organization. Of course these topics are not the only ones; we may have overlooked others so use this chapter to help think through what's important in your own career. Talk to other more experienced managers, men or women, in your organization and ask them for their advice. You don't necessarily need a detailed, step by step, account of each career move they made along the way; it's more about some of the broader issues; what would they have done differently and what would have helped them progress their career? Learn from their experiences and expertise.

As mentioned earlier, if you are unlucky enough to have a poor boss take heart as it does also offer an advantage. Use your time to learn about what it is they are doing that you would not do. One or two of our interviewees have been through this experience, *'she was the boss* *from hell' – 'I learned as much in my early career from a bad boss about how **not to** do things as I did from when I had the opportunity to work for a good boss.'*

HR directors and chief executives could (and should) create more opportunities for exchanging career advice. A women leadership program, for example, is one way to do this; another is a women's network as happens at Google UK. Someone involved in a women's network elsewhere comments on what happened when the chief executive came along to talk, discuss, listen and answer any questions – *'I found his honesty and advice so valuable. He would discuss any subject and we learnt so much. He'd answer any question we put to him and if he didn't know the answer we pretty soon heard back from him after the meeting.'* Another point about this story is that the chief executive's personal involvement sent a strong message to his senior team and the rest of the company about the value of the network.

A positive company attitude can make all the difference – Danish pharmaceutical company Novo Nordisk for example includes a statement about diversity on its website,

> We have had a diversity strategy since 2009, which includes the aspiration that within five years all senior management teams must be diverse in terms of gender and nationality.
>
> From Novo Nordisk Annual Report 2010;
http://annualreport2010.novonordisk.com/
default.aspx accessed July 2011.

The aim of this chapter is to highlight an individual's own ability to change and improve which, when combined with support from others and a bit of planning, can help you progress your career.

Of course it's not only about you, the individual. Remembering to keep family and friends on-side is also important. There's little point in achieving what you want from your career if it's at the expense of your family and friends. Another dimension is about those who work with you. Not everyone appreciates how much of a manager's reputation is affected by the qualities of those surrounding them. Our advice is to think about the value of creating the very best team you can around you. It's a point mentioned by a number of the women leaders we interviewed who say this has been, and continues to be, an important component of their success.

I have a great team and I make a point to tell them so – they work extraor-dinarily hard and they really are an ace team, they are arguably one of the best around. I give them a lot of credit publicly for their work and I also tell them how good they are.

Interview quote

If you want to be seen by others as an effective leader you need an effective, motivated team who believes in you. And, as the quote at the start of this chapter from Gillian Hibberd highlights, look for indi-viduals whom you trust. Organizational politics can be tricky and it helps a good deal to know your own team is loyal.

So, is this chapter relevant to you? Those of you already at senior levels maybe feel no need to read any further. You probably have a clear idea of what you want – or will shortly achieve e.g., the key job, management level, recognition, whatever it might be. However, you still have a role in helping change the future for other younger women who are just beginning their career. It's not just what happens in the organization where you work or in your professional association, or role models to encourage younger women; it's also about external links. Any opportunity you have to speak to women students either at schools or colleges can make a difference. A recent example is the link which Michelle Obama created by her UK visit in 2009, and subsequent encouragement, to girls at the Elizabeth Garrett Anderson college.[1] Selecting an inner-city school in London that was not A-listed, her visit was intended to help inspire the girls to achieve more, to appreciate that being clever, achieving a great education, is cool. See guardian. co.uk/education/2009/apr/05/michelle-obama-school-london to read more about this. On a return visit early in 2011 she accompanied the girls on a day visit to Oxford University, again with the purpose of helping raise their sights about what they could achieve. www.ox.ac. uk/media/news_stories/2011/112505.html

A great corporate event between seven competitor companies is the **Connecting Women in Technology** Conference which is organized each year by senior women managers in Google, IBM, Dell, Microsoft, Intel, HP and Cisco. Around 200 women attended the 2011 conference in the UK. Sarah Speake, Strategic Marketing Director from Google UK, is one of the volunteers who organizes the event and says that everyone involved gives their time over and above their busy day jobs because they think the conference is a useful resource to support and encourage other women.

The impact and practical value of real life stories is clear. The video of the US conference, see URL link below, highlights the 'best career advice' from Madeleine Albright[2] (a few other highlights are also noted) and other speakers at the Women's Conference, an annual event hosted in California by Maria Shriver. It's an amazing conference and all the speakers featured in the video offer good advice; a particular favorite is Dr Jane Goodall who remembers what her mother told her. At a time when others laughed at her crazy dream to go and work with animals in Africa, her mother said *'never, never give up.'* Her life and achievements are in a very different sphere to the business world but the principles are the same and can help anyone achieve their career goals. General information and video content about the conference can be found either on YouTube or on the conference website (the first event happened in 2003). www.youtube.com/user/thewomensconference and www.womensconference.org accessed July 2011.

A few extracts from 'Best career advice' from Madeleine Albright and other speakers at the Women's Conference are given below:

> *Enjoy everything that you do…*
> *Listen to your heart…*
> *If you want to create change you do not ask anyone for permission…*

Some people say that *'well, it was difficult for me to achieve my career aspirations and so it should be for the next generation of women'*. It's a poor approach in our view – look rather for ways to make life better, simpler and easier for those who travel behind you. Anyone involved in leadership programs – either as an organizer or participant – could easily create video YouTube clips of advice from delegates.

So let's take a closer look at each of the four areas in the diagram we showed you earlier, four different themes of career advice. The first one is personal skill development.

THEME 1: PERSONAL SKILL DEVELOPMENT

Confidence in your own ability

A good deal depends on your own confidence. But how do you know how good you are? It can be hard to gauge how much difference you do make if no one in your team gives you any feedback, or maybe you only get feedback from your boss when things go wrong, so it's hard to assess your contribution objectively. So make a point of regularly asking for feedback and take time to reflect on how you might have improved a task or project. Make sure you are also clear about what makes you good (this is where a mentor or coach can be really helpful). That doesn't mean you should create impossibly high standards for yourself – make sure you are realistic in your assessment. Feedback from others should also help you with this process.

Most people do better in an environment where they feel appreciated and valued and there's no doubt that working for a good boss is a significant ingredient in this recipe. You might like to consider the approach taken by one woman leader we interviewed who says that throughout her multinational career it's been the qualities and attitude of the boss, rather than any job, which is the most important consideration when making a new move. As she explains,

> It's the line manager who is critical to your career. I've been very aware of this throughout my career and have often chosen a job because it gave me the chance to work for a good manager – you can change the job later, rather than focusing only on what the job is. My advice to women is that they should find good managers. It's so important for your career development. You can look at a very attractive job but if the line manager is not likely to be supportive then don't touch it because you just set yourself up for failure. I've seen it happen. Whereas sometimes a job that actually doesn't look very interesting but has a really good line manager means that you can make that job what you need it to be.

> I had one bad experience with a line manager and since then I used that policy – I have consciously not applied for, or not accepted, jobs because of the line manager. It's made a huge difference to the quality of my life and more so to my own development, because I've managed to establish really good relationships with my line managers. This means they're happier to give you time and flexibility and they're more interested to actually develop you and as a result I've got a lot out of every job.

A similar point is made in another part of the world by Yao Hong, Vice President at China Post. She gets on well with her manager and says that she freely shares ideas with him and thinks *'that this is one of my key success factors, which is why I believe that I have had a relatively smooth career.'*

One way to improve your own ability is to be certain you are knowledgeable and keep up to date with what's going on across the rest of the business. Another person we interviewed in a multinational highlights the need to know the business so well that you can always understand in detail how decisions taken by your department/business area, etc., will impact on everyone else. That way you have credibility with others in the senior team. And as someone else explains, networking can play a key role here:

> *I often talk with individuals in the team who are not in my direct management line. A lot of these are personal contacts and as the result of the initial start-up phase are people who joined early on in the process. We were all there at the start and so working closely together at that time means we have some close bonds and have built a lot of trust. These conversations can be really helpful for keeping my finger on the pulse of what's happening across the business teams.*

Interview quote

Getting to know yourself

If the words 'know yourself' sound a bit light and frothy or too much like a 'motherhood and apple pie' statement then please take time to reconsider. It is this advice by far which we heard most often during our research. The other most frequently mentioned advice, is about confidence. One woman leader we interviewed speaks about the importance of *'authentic leadership'*:

> *When I was younger I would change my style often. I was too much like a chameleon – I was a young woman manager working in the technology sector and so I tried to be one type of leader when I was with older, male colleagues and another, different type of person when I was with younger colleagues. Now I am more conscious about authentic leadership and the value of being myself. So if you ask my boss, my team or any of my colleagues or my family they will all describe me in the same way. That was certainly not true at the start of my career.*

Sarah Speake,
Strategic Marketing Director, Google

122

As we get older we usually move closer towards expressing our own values, our own leadership values and behaviors – whatever makes good sense to us. And perhaps we are less inclined to try and behave in the way others expect us to behave – something that has been a problem for many young women managers wanting to 'fit in' when they are in a minority in the workplace or in a management team. A number of comments were made on this topic including the following:

Find a balance of what you enjoy and what you are good at and combine the two.

Work out what your strengths are and play to them.

Another powerful comment made by a number of women was said a number of times, and in many situations – *the world is your oyster.* **(Interview quotes)**

Look out for opportunities to attend leadership development programs – they are a great way to get feedback and also provide an opportunity to understand more about different types of leadership style. In one multinational which ran a series of women-only programs a high proportion, nearly a third of the group, from the first five programs (through to July 2010) went on to win promotion. In a major financial services group over 75 percent of those who attended the Ashridge custom-made program were later promoted. If your organization does not offer any leadership training in-house then consult with your boss and others to find something externally which will suit you or design your own custom-made package.

Three points to bear in mind that may help with increasing your knowledge of yourself and your leadership style:

- **Self-knowledge:** Look at different ways to build your self-awareness e.g., tools such as the Myers Briggs Type Indicator and 360-degree feedback are useful here. It's even better if everyone in the business uses the same process e.g., the following example describes the approach in one multinational:

We have an annual 360-Degree Feedback process for executives and managers across all businesses. The process is focused on building self-awareness by linking results to a best-in-class personality assessment inventory (the Hogan Assessment Suite). The process requires mandatory follow-up feedback meetings with certified professionals (based on a custom-designed three-day certification program) in the 360-Degree Feedback process, along with personality tools to ensure a high-quality and rigorous feedback and development planning discussion.

■ **Honest feedback and learning:** Remember to keep on learning – some managers get to a level (or age) where they think there no longer is any need to reflect. There's also a danger that as you become more senior people will flatter you too much and not feel comfortable to tell you the unvarnished truth. You need to have an open mind that welcomes such honest feedback from others; Amy Nelson-Bennett[3] describes how attitudes towards her changed when she was promoted to CEO at the beauty product company Molton Brown. She needed to remind colleagues not to treat her any differently from how they had done before when she was in charge of marketing – *'I don't have a disease.'*

■ **Consider your sphere of influence:** Think carefully about your impact and influence. In the 4th century BC the Greek writer and soldier Xenophon advised leaders not to misuse the power they have and it's advice that is still relevant for business leaders in the 21st century (some of his other views also seem quite modern, he wrote for example about how not to get fat!)

THEME 2: CAREER PLANNING AND PROCESSES

Look one job ahead all the time

Women sometimes focus on the job in hand at the expense of planning ahead so try to think about looking forward, one job ahead all the time; it's a point that was mentioned a number of times during our research. What we mean here is good, old-fashioned career planning – look at where you are now – is it where you want to be? Look beyond your current task and ask yourself where you wish to be in the next year or so. Write a career plan and keep it up-to-date. See Chapter 9 for ideas. Often, when people settle into a role or make a new move that's quite challenging the career plan is neglected until the next time it's needed. But there's always the unexpected: if tomorrow you are unexpectedly looking for a new job or asked to put forward your CV or résumé to be considered for a key project team somewhere else in the company, it's much easier to do this with the latest information about your key achievements, project assignments, etc.

You may like to think about the GROW model. This has been used in UK coaching since the early 1990s and although it was developed for sports coaching it is equally useful in helping you to think about your career plan. See www.insideoutdev.com/site/ip_grow_model for more information.

If you are a dual-career couple it obviously makes sense for you both to look at career plans together. What are the important decisions for the next few years? Is one career likely to be achieved at the expense of the other? Is there a quiet time, some down-time, for one partner (say when the children are young)? Situation can help too – some of the women we interviewed have a partner who can work from home. Is one career phase (say taking an MBA) likely to create problems for both of you and if you identify potential problems what will help you both to cope?

Moving from middle to senior management often represents a big step up in terms of skills and responsibilities. If you are working in a large corporation you may like to think about the differences between the management levels – see table for an example from one multinational. If this isn't available then create your own framework and test it out with colleagues and others.

Key skills for different management levels (Note: the same skills are expected for junior and middle managers but with greater scope, etc. expected from middle managers.)

Junior and Middle Manager	Senior Manager
Experience/success in different areas across the functions	Cross-divisional assignment
Field operating assignment	International assignment/s
Head office assignment	Significant change leadership
Start-up e.g., new sales channel, line plant	Cross-function experience
Building and executing a strategy	Coach/mentor of others
Fix-it e.g., turnaround/restructuring	
Building a team	
Special project/task force	

THEME 3: RELATIONSHIPS

Find a sponsor

A mentor and a coach will also help your career but as a number of women comment, a sponsor is vital. It's a slightly different role as a sponsor is someone who acts as an advocate for you, and promotes your abilities to others in the organization.

The value of a sponsor is that they are partisan – they are already convinced you are good; they feel comfortable in promoting your abilities and talents to others and, even more practically, will look for ways to help you make an impact. One way to do this is to consider 'small wins' either in terms of project outputs or team goals. (By the way this does not contradict the point made in the next section about the value of audacious goals for teams – you can do both.) You may already have personal experience of the value of 'small wins' but if not, then think about some managers you admire as it's likely they know the value of this approach. Sponsors can also help you think about what are the 'small wins' (with big impact) that will help you and your team.

Illustration: The value of a quick win

A powerful example of 'small wins' with big impact is Rudy Giuliani's approach which was widely reported at the time. As the newly appointed Mayor of New York City in the 1990s he needed to deliver on his promise to reduce crime. But such a vast issue and such high levels of crime were daunting for everyone involved; where on earth could he start without having to wait years before seeing some positive change? He realized that the 'squeegee men' were a good place to begin. These people haunted road junctions (as happens in many other cities) and dashed out to wash the windscreen when cars pulled up, and then intimidated drivers by demanding cash. On the scale of serious crime it wasn't the worst but it was a problem that everyone (except the squeegee men) disliked. It needed some creative thinking as well as a bit of legal knowledge to tackle the problem but they found a way to stop it – the first success of many; it was also an action that was hugely popular among New Yorkers. See Rudy Giuliani's Leadership book[4] to read more about this story.

Many of the women we interviewed talk about the power of sponsorship and how it's helped them as highlighted in the box that follows:

126

The power of sponsorship: Support, challenge and grow

Tang Fajin was General Manager (the most senior job) in the area company where one of the women leaders we interviewed was working. She had not been there long and as she explains he played a key role in her development as a leader – *'Tang Fajin was the first person to recognize my potential and to give me the opportunity to take on more responsibilities. It was my first management role and I had moved from my original work in the trade union area to take an HR role. When I had achieved my first tasks I went to see him, expecting to be praised for the work I had done... I knew that the work was well done but he didn't give me any praise. Instead he set me more challenging objectives that he knew would stretch me further. It was a valuable lesson as it showed me how much more I could achieve.'* She emphasizes that without a push she would not have achieved as much and it was only later that she recognized the value of his approach.

The words above are from Guimei Pan, who is a senior Vice-President at Sinopec, one of the world's largest oil companies. In 2009 Sinopec became the first Chinese corporation among the Top Ten of the Fortune Global 500. Madame Pan, as she is known within the company, joined in the early 1980s when she was 23. As the eldest child in the family she decided that going to work (rather than continuing with her education) would help her parents and in particular her salary would help support the education of her younger brother and sister. Her first job was as a junior employee in Sinopec's area company in Hunan Province and she expected little promotion which at that time was the usual career path. Instead, she has risen to the most senior level of Sinopec despite the fact that she did not set out with any ambitions about how to manage her career.

I don't think about my next job now, nor did I when I first started work – I will do whatever is in the interest of the company; that's my guiding principle. I'm lucky that my efforts have been rewarded.

THEME 4: ORGANIZATIONAL ISSUES

Build the best team around you

Getting the day job done in a pressured environment often means managers focus on the immediate task in hand and find it hard to move beyond 'fire-fighting'. However, it's also important to find time to look objectively at team quality if you are to build the very best team around you. Think about the following questions (see table):

Build the best team around you

How good is your team?	If you think it's really good, would all your colleagues and your clients agree?
	What processes could improve what you do?
	Where are their weaknesses?
	Do you tell the team how good they are?
Is there a team somewhere that's better?	What do they do that you don't?
	What needs to happen to make your team better?
	Think about the way Guimei Pan was encouraged – in the box above – and look at ways to support, challenge and grow individuals, and the team

Rudy Giuliani is a clever leader and so it's not surprising to find one of the chapters in his Leadership book is *'surround yourself with great people'*. We also heard from many of the women we interviewed that a good team is clearly important and is part of what has helped them be successful. Or, to think about this another way, it's much harder to be a good leader if you are trying to manage a poor team all pulling in different directions or maybe you have a few passengers who are not pulling their weight at all! So whether you lead your own team or are a member of different project teams think about what the team currently does and how to improve team dynamics.

Some leaders worry about delegating to others in their team, concerned that this may lessen their power and authority. Good leaders however recognize that it's a key way to raise standards of performance –

I'm a great delegator and I never worry about being somewhere if someone else who was capable was available to go in my place. Many managers have a huge insecurity about this but I never did; I think it's also a great way to develop people. I've always made savvy decisions about where I spend my time. We've all seen colleagues who try to be everywhere at once and to deal with every-thing – it's not possible to work like this, meetings are not productive and you can see the impact; they don't pay full attention to those working for them.

She has little patience for those who say *'I can do it faster myself', 'it's usually nonsense and then there's the stress it creates. Delegation should be a standard approach in how you manage your team.'*

Interview quote

128

Another factor in building a good team is the skill in how you set goals, in particular about setting high goals. Sir Terry Leahy, one of the UK's most respected chief executives, describes a number of issues that helped him transform Tesco from a relatively small supermarket into a major world player – one of these is setting *'audacious goals'*. The impact of such targets, he says, really motivates people who are always capable of more than they think.[5] Consider your own performance – and about your team – and think about how often you set challenging targets.

REFLECTIVE EXERCISE

If you want to build a great team think about the following statements.

Exercise: Creating More Effective Teams

	True	False
Communications		
Team managers (or all the team if it's a small group of people) meet regularly e.g., weekly on the same day and time		
One on one meetings are regularly held with all individual team members (weekly, maybe daily or on a rolling system of frequency)		
Papers and key information are always circulated before team meetings		
Responsibility		
An 'action list' of 'who will do what by when' is circulated after every team meeting		
No-one is left to struggle alone e.g., when there are unexpected deadlines or problems everyone helps out		
There is a high level of trust and respect among members of the team		
Everyone in the team is committed and motivated to create an outstanding team		
Everyone in the team is clear about: their own objectives the team's objectives the business objectives		
Audacious goals (for both team and in the business) are set		

(Continued)

	True	False
Skills and development		
A good 'learning exchange' atmosphere exists within the team e.g., individuals mentor one another passing on skills and expert knowledge		
Process		
Time is spent in business meetings to consider how team members can help one another be more effective and how the team can be more effective to clients		
Any newcomer to the team can quickly understand behaviors that are important for team members e.g., as a result of a workshop to identify key values, behaviors and issues and a summary published of exactly what good (and bad) looks like		

SUMMARY

Everyone needs support and help from others in order to achieve their potential. And whatever your current job role or management level, think about your skills; look for ways to capitalize on your strengths; look for ways to address any weaknesses.

We have not discussed much in this chapter about gender – is our advice relevant only for women? Some issues are gender neutral but there are certain differences. One example is confidence – women are sometimes held back by a lack of confidence, a lack of self belief and so thinking about this and finding out your own capabilities are particularly useful exercises. As one woman we interviewed said, knowing that she was good early on in her career would have made a significant difference.

Sponsorship also has a gender dimension. Yes, it is relevant for both men and women but women – especially those moving into middle management levels – are likely to gain more from having someone more senior who will act as their sponsor in the organization. This is because they may be one of the few women at this level and may therefore feel more of an 'outsider' – a sponsor can help them move quickly towards being an 'insider'.

And as one person points out, *'going ahead, diving in and failing isn't so bad – so long as you learn from the mistakes. The biggest failure is not taking any risk and not going at all.'* (**Interview quote**)

(Continued)

Better support, and better opportunities, in a positive working environment would help more women to acquire the experience that will help them in more senior leadership roles.

Women need the environment where they can just jump in and try something.

Survey quote

Words of Advice – the final comments in this chapter (survey quotes, presented in bubbles) are quotes from the women involved in our research who when they reflect on their own career offer plenty of words of wisdom. An interesting theme that a number of people highlight is to find work that you enjoy – by the way this isn't a comment just from entrepreneurs but is also said by those in large private sector firms and those working for the public sector.

Be strong and stick to your guns

Be bold and confident. Try out new challenges and don't be afraid of learning and failing occasionally

Embrace and enjoy change – I can't say that I personally have always liked change but now I do because as soon as there is change there are also opportunities. There's always going to be change so why not embrace it?

Choose what you can really excel at and never turn back

Be confident/tough/work hard, keep fighting, be fearless, believe in yourself, don't be afraid of failure

Keep fighting, it's worth it

Be confident in your capabilities

Women do sometimes suffer from the 'imposter syndrome' but they need to get over this, and simply have a go at different jobs and different challenges. The men will just go for it and jump in and if women want to compete on the same terms then they simply must just hold their noses and dive in too and not confess to anyone about their imposter syndrome feeling. Men sometimes feel the same too but they don't admit it

Anything is possible if you believe in yourself

Be very clear about what you would like to achieve and at which 'cost'

Explore what is important to you personally and what you value in your life

Be honest with yourself about what you want

Be true to your own values

Know yourself/strengths and weaknesses/values/follow your heart/pursue your dreams/ be true to yourself/plan your career carefully

Stay true to yourself – you only have the one life and ensure you live it rather than wishing for something else

Be authentic to yourself, pursue your dreams and never give up, no matter what others say

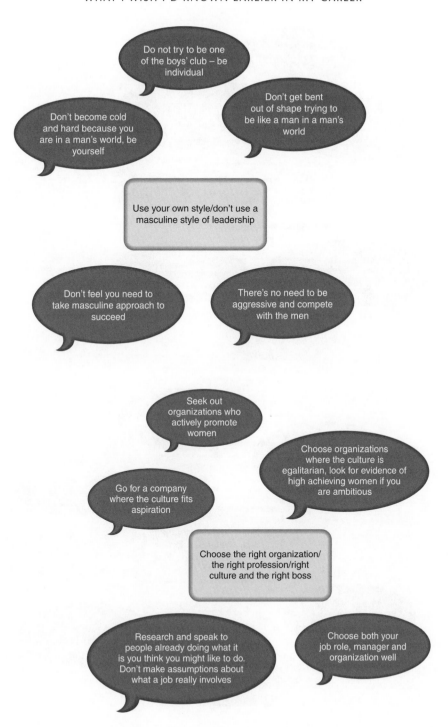

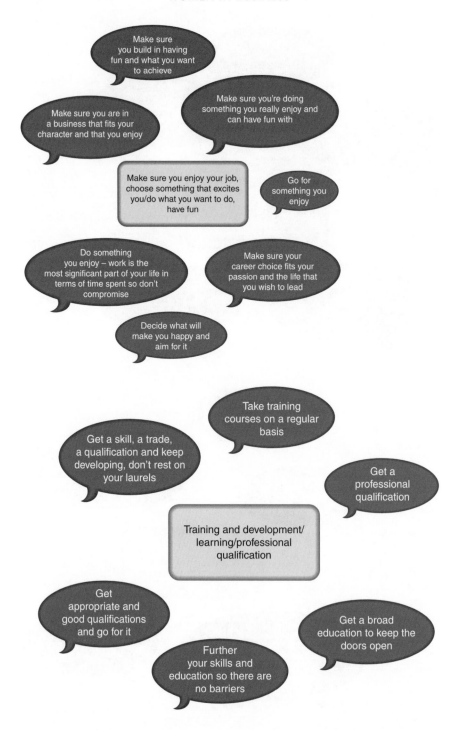

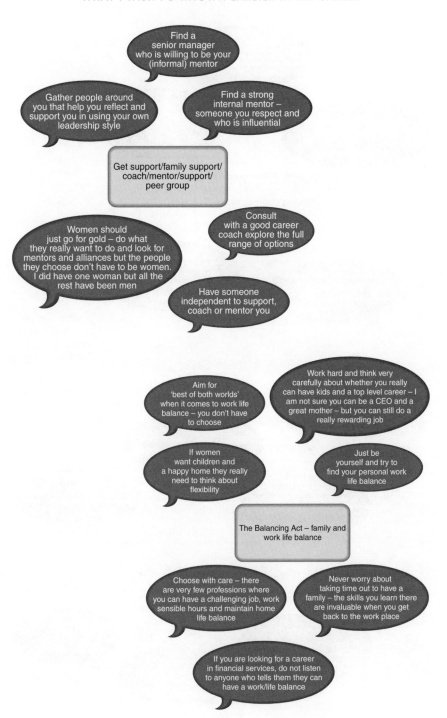

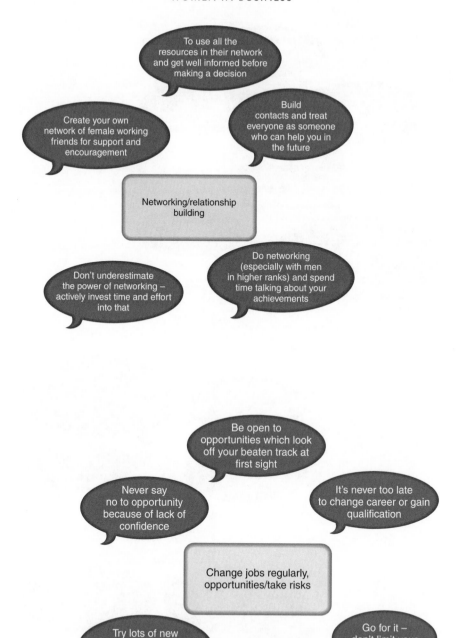

Seize the opportunities

And a final thought which applies regardless of management level, age or career stage

9

STRATEGIES FOR CAREER SUCCESS

If you are not pushing your career, nobody's going to be dragging you along.

Interview quote

As you have seen from previous chapters one vital area highlighted is the benefit of having a career strategy. Many women indicated that in hindsight they wished they had the benefit of having such a plan earlier in their career.

In today's complex business world individuals can no longer rely on organizations to provide them with a job for life or indeed to reward hard work and loyalty with promotion. Today you must become responsible for your own career management. The organization, bosses, family, friends and others in your relationship network will be there to provide support and in some cases opportunities but the reality is that you are the architect of your own career.

WHY IS IT IMPORTANT?

It is important to recognize and understand that no one else can manage your career better than you can. Yes, other people can contribute but taking responsibility, developing your own plans and making your own decisions is liberating, exciting and necessary to navigate today's career world. Some people are lucky and achieve a lot without a plan but we believe these people are in the minority. Many of those who succeed talk about goals, dreams, plans and of course a little bit of luck.

Having a plan and knowing what you want to achieve at various stages in your life does not have to be restrictive – plans are made to help you to move in the right direction and do not need to be rigidly applied. A bit like a route map – this will help you reach your destination but it is always possible to deviate from the route to do something of interest along the way (see the following illustration).

A process for career success

```
┌─────────────────────────────────────────────────────┐
│              Career strategy plan                      │
└─────────────────────────────────────────────────────┘
                          │
                          ▼
            ┌─────────────────────────────┐
            │   My career aspirations      │
            │ • Your dream job or career   │
            └─────────────────────────────┘
```

What	Who	How
• Education	• Relationships	• Preparation
• Training	• Mentors	• Personal brand
• Time line	• Coaches	• Self promotion
so far in life	• Role models	
• Successes	• Networks	
• Skills	• Internal	
• Development	• External	
needs	• Professional	
	• Social	

```
            ┌─────────────────────────────┐
            │      My career plan          │
            │  •   The route map           │
            └─────────────────────────────┘
```

In order to create this career strategy you might find it useful to get yourself a blank notebook or create a file on your computer or IPad which you can use to work through various processes, jot down notes and develop ideas and plans. It doesn't matter whether you are a lists sort of person or a pictures sort of person; you will still need to capture your ideas. When you write things down it tends to help you to focus and develop clarity. Writing it down also gives you a structure and route map to follow. You should also review your plan regularly to check you are on track and to make any changes which might be appropriate based on your situation at any point in time.

Life has a habit of following a non linear process and often the most exciting opportunities come along out of the blue and when we least expect them. Knowing what your goals and plans are when this type of situation occurs will help you to make informed decisions. For instance, more than one respondent to our questionnaire talked about the benefits associated with getting international experience early in their career. For many this hadn't been something they had actively considered and were certainly not planning to work abroad; however, for those who took advantage of the opportunity it tended to pay dividends in the long run. For some it didn't mean promotion or more money – often it was at some personal disadvantage, however, no one reported that international experience was a hindrance to their career. One of our interviewees highlighted the importance of international experience *'the chance to travel – especially early on in your career – is a chance to inform your views and meet a much wider set of people. I was very fortunate that I was able to do this in my first job with Morgan Stanley and I'd definitely recommend it to others'.*

Some of the processes that follow will help you to review, analyze and reflect upon your career so far and get you started on the process of planning the way ahead.

MY CAREER STRATEGY – CAREER ASPIRATIONS

There is a popular saying which suggests that those people who have something to aim at are more likely to achieve their goal than those who simply drift through life. One of our interviewees told us that her career aspiration was to *'become a board director by the time I was 30'* and she went on to explain how she managed to achieve this! Having an idea of your career aspirations, goals and even dreams will give you something to aim for. So, ask yourself:

- What professional area am I interested in e.g., Human Resources, Information Technology, Legal, Finance, etc?
- What type of organization would I like to work for, e.g., Public Sector or Private Sector, Voluntary Sector, Large International Organization, Small Local Organization, Start Up, etc.?
- What would my ideal boss be like?
- What level of seniority would I like to get to?
- Am I more interested to pursue a career in General Management or Technical/Professional track?

- Is self employment of interest?
- Do I want to manage others?

Once you have a general idea of your future aspirations you might like to summarize these into a short personal mission statement. For instance, *my goal is to become a PR Director for a large multinational. During my journey to this dream I would like to gain experience with a PR agency, work in an international context and eventually manage my own PR team*. The steps below offer a range of ideas, thoughts and tools to help you manage your career.

MY CAREER STRATEGY – WHAT

Education and training are two areas of key importance for your career development strategy. Many of the women we interviewed and those who responded to our survey indicated that having the right qualifications had been key to their success. For instance, *'My decision to study at university in spite of negative advice'*, *'I believe having the education, degree, masters, etc is the one thing that really supported my career, by giving me total credibility'* and *'I gained an Open Business School MBA following six long years of part time study. The education matched my career progression and gave me the theoretical training along-side my job'*. **(Survey quotes)**

Qualifications are great, whether you get them in the traditional way or whether you study part time while also working; and it is important to align your career aspirations with your studies. But formal qualifications are not the only form of education that will help in your career. Less formal education and training often referred to as the 'university of life' should also be considered when thinking about this area. So, for instance, give consideration to internships, voluntary work, secondments and job shadowing as ways of developing your capabilities and experience.

Taking advantage of any training opportunities offered to you will also be beneficial – short courses, online seminars, podcasts, technical training and of course all the various ways of getting training through observation, practice and grabbing opportunities to try out new skills and take on new challenges when they are offered. Many professional bodies encourage their members to keep a journal of continuing profes-sional development and this is certainly a great way to record and analyze what you are learning, how you are learning it and how you can use this learning in your day-to-day life. So, if you are a member of a professional body it is worth looking at their website to see what's offered in this area – you may well get some extra tips. If you work in a small organization with limited formal development opportunities find a mentor. Also, look at what's available in print and think about management journals (a few examples are noted in the table that follows for different countries). We're not saying you must know about every management idea in detail but a regular scan will ensure you keep up to date with new ideas and help broaden your horizons.

Management publications

Austria	Magazin Training and also some of the main newspapers offer weekend special reports on management topics, e.g., *DiePresse, Der Standard*
Belgium	In Belgium there is no dedicated management magazine but the most widely read is probably a magazine called *Trends*
Germany	*Manager Seminare* and the German edition of HBR. In German speaking countries (including Austria and parts of Switzerland) *Personalwirtschaft* is considered a leading journal
Holland	*Management Team* and *Quote*, and of course the daily newspaper *Financieele Dagblad*, the equivalent of Il Sole24Ore and the *Financial Times* HH
International	*Harvard Business Review* (HBR)
Italy	*L'Impresa* is Italy's biggest management magazine and appears monthly in one of the major newspapers Il Sole24Ore
Sweden	*Dagens Industry* is a daily business magazine that many business people read. If it's a leadership or HR issue then *Ledarskap* is also read by those in the HR community.
Switzerland	*NZZ* newspaper and also some of the main newspapers offer weekend special reports and also online
UK	*Management Today, The Financial Times* and the *Director*

In many ways what we are suggesting in this chapter is going a step further and focusing on your whole career in addition to your development, so that you have an understanding of what you are good at, what you are not so good at, what you have done so far in your life and your ideas about development for the future. The following practical tools can all be useful to help you in this process.

Career strategy tools time line

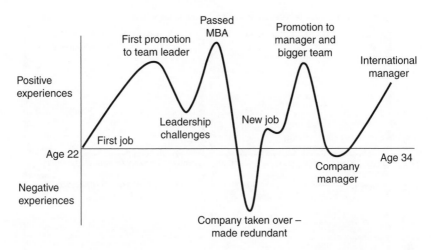

Create your own time line and annotate it with your life and career highs and lows. The time line can be as detailed as you wish. It can focus only on career, only on life or both. You can also choose the time period on which you wish to focus. From this simple exercise you can begin to see where and when you are most happy and, of course, when you are not. You may also find it useful to discuss this chart with your coach or mentor. Talking something like this through can identify even more information that can be useful in developing your career strategy.

Personal SWOT analysis

One of the easiest self-analysis tools is to apply the classic SWOT analysis to yourself. Start by drawing the two-by-two box chart (see below) on a sheet of paper and then think about and note down all those attributes you consider to be your strengths; then focus on what you believe to be your weaknesses. Once you have a feeling for your strengths and weaknesses you should then look externally to determine any opportunities available to you and any threats that may prove to be barriers or hurdles in your career progress. Note it all down in the SWOT chart or on a separate sheet of paper.

Personal SWOT analysis

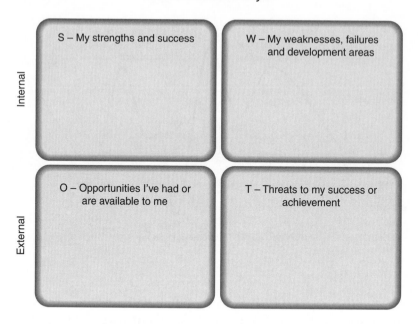

It is best to take a while to complete this exercise. Our lives and careers are complex and it is important to gather all the relevant data. You might also like to discuss this with others to help you identify your strengths and weaknesses and the full range of opportunities and threats that you may face.

The next exercise is a bit more structured and involves a skill or competence analysis. Many of these types of assessment can be found on the Internet – the one we are using is based on research done at Ashridge about the key competences or skills a leader requires. Our list is not exhaustive and you may find that there are other competences that are important for your particular job role and environment. If this is the case simply use the same assessment criteria to gather the data most relevant for your situation.

Complete the analysis by assessing your current skill level for each of the competences. It is also important to assess what you believe to be the importance level of each competence for either your current role or more importantly for your career future. If you would like to take part in the Ashridge research in this area check this link – http://www.ashridge.org.uk/leadership-importance

Skill/Competence Analysis

Competence/Skill description	Skill level 1 (Low)–5 (High)	Importance 1 (Low)–5 (High)
Personal skills		
Adaptable – flexibility to adjust your approach, language and views to suit differing situations		
Decisive – willing to take risks and make tough or quick decisions, to commit to a course of action and be accountable for the outcome		
Innovative – demonstrates an enquiring mind and encourages new ideas		
Personally effective – ability to change, prioritize and use time effectively, know impact you have on others		
Problem solver – identifies issues, gathers all relevant information, interprets the facts and explores all possible solutions		
Self developer – takes responsibility and control for own development and learning and plans for the future		
Self management – demonstrates integrity, self confidence and assertiveness in a variety of business situations		
Interpersonal skills		
Communicator – communicates ideas and information in a clear, concise and open manner appropriate to the audience		
Development oriented – creates an environment that ensures people have the right skills and knowledge and encourages their development		
Influencer – works with others to gain commitment and agreement to ideas and action		

(Continued)

145

Competence/Skill description	Skill level 1 (Low)–5 (High)	Importance 1 (Low)–5 (High)
Manages others – leads, encourages and supports the work of others to achieve their objectives in the most effective way		
Manages performance – sets clear and realistic goals, monitors performance, acts on under performance, gives feedback and is committed to continuous improvement		
Politically sensitive – understands agendas and perspectives of others, recognises and balances the needs of the group and the broader organization		
Teamworker – pro-actively co-operates and interacts with others for the benefit of the team and the business		
Business skills		
Business acumen – ability to understand the way the organization runs, its external environment and uses this knowledge to improve performance		
Financial awareness – understands the concepts of profit and loss, cash flow and managing budgets in order to use financial information effectively		
Information manager – makes available meaningful and accurate information to enable timely fact based decisions and process improvement		
Marketing awareness – understands basic marketing principles in order to set up a system to tap into customer needs and market moves		
Process manager – understands the principles of how a business operates, both on a day-to-day and longer-term basis and seeks to encourage performance improvement		

(Continued)

Competence/Skill description	Skill level 1 (Low)–5 (High)	Importance 1 (Low)–5 (High)
Technology awareness – understands the impact of technology on their business environment and how to exploit it for improved performance		
Strategic skills		
Change oriented – understands the need for and implications of change in the organizational context and acts as a change agent		
Cultural awareness – understands different cultures within the organization and outside and adapts behavior in order to get things done in unfamiliar environments		
Leadership orientation – creates vision, has integrity, influences and motivates others to perform effectively		
Socially responsible – creates a culture that is productive and socially responsible		
Strategic perspective – has the capacity to see the big picture, how different issues are related to each other, the structure in a situation or process and the ability to understand the long-term implications		

Once you have assessed your skills you can now begin to develop a greater understanding of your strengths, weaknesses and development needs. By analyzing your skill level and assessing the importance of each skill for your current role or for your career future, you can begin to develop a plan for the future.

A comparison of strengths, weaknesses and importance levels will reveal information about your preferences and help you to identify where you need to develop for future success.

Summary of skill/competence analysis

Strengths and weaknesses	Importance
Note down your major strengths where you have scored 4 or 5.	Note down all the skills you believe to be of significant importance for your career success – items where you have scored 4 or 5
Note down any weaknesses where you have scored 1 or 2	Note down all the skills you believe to be unimportant for your career success – scores of 1 or 2.
Note down those skills where you score 3 – neither a strength or weakness.	Note down all the skills where you scored 3 – the skills that are neither important to or unimportant for your career success
Key messages emerging about skills to develop.	

Now you can analyze the data and begin to draw meaning from it. So for instance if all your strengths are all 'important' then you are on the right track. However, if all your strengths bear little relation to the important skills you will have to work to develop these new skills and

148

abilities to be better prepared for future success or possibly you may need to change direction.

In addition to skill and competence analysis you may also like to review and make notes about the information you have gathered from any other psychometric questionnaires or personality inventories that you have completed. All this information is useful to help you understand yourself, to develop your confidence and to build self belief.

MY CAREER STRATEGY – WHO

No one is alone in this process. As one of our interviewees commented *'you need a good peer group around you – both internally and also outside of the organisation. It's been a massive help to me in my career. It's so important to have a network – a group of allies – around you who you can talk to at different stages in your career, who you can be open and honest with about how you are feeling.'* You need to understand who can help you to achieve your career dreams, ambitions and goals. One way of doing this is to create a Network chart as shown below.

Network chart

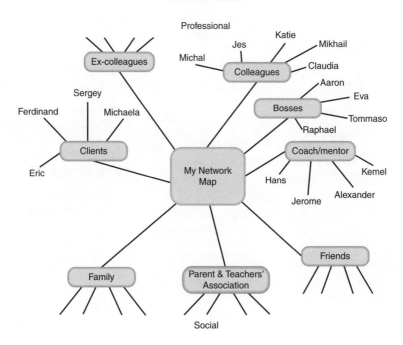

Now that you have created your chart (usually it will need much more space than the chart above – at least an A4 sheet) you can see all the people you believe might be able to help you – the next stage of this part of the process is to annotate your network map to indicate:

- How each of these people came into your life, at what stage in your life, how long have you known them
- The role that each person has played in your career so far – identify who has been a coach, mentor, role model, colleague, etc.
- Those people who are best placed to help with your career
- The role that you would like these people to play in the future
- The quality of your relationship with these people
- Are there other people who you would like to appear on your network map?

Network map

Jes
- New colleague (1 year)
- Pretty distant
- Very quiet
- Develop further

Katie
- Closest colleague (5 years)
- Confidante
- Supportive
- Encourage to challenge

Michal
- Oldest colleague (10 years)
- Friend
- Good devil's advocate
- Supporter

Colleagues

Mikhail
- Worked together for 3 years
- Straight talker
- Influential with boss
- Challenger

Claudia
- Worked together for 7 years
- Quiet
- Hard worker
- Introvert

My Network Map

When analyzing these data it is useful to reflect on the networks and how the various relationships were developed and the value of these relationships to you. In particular those people you develop relationships with early in your life at school, college, university and first jobs often form the basis of lifelong friendships and alliances that are built on trust, shared experience and respect. They often become those people in your network that you depend upon throughout your life to be devil's advocate, wise counsel and to provide a general listening ear when you are faced with challenges, disappointments and opportunities in both your career and your life.

Today there is much written about the power of social networks for all sorts of supportive reasons, and we suspect most of you will be signed up on Facebook, LinkedIn, Friends Reunited or some other social network. Signing up isn't enough; it's about making your networks work for you and understanding who in these networks are the most useful. Respondents to our questionnaire often commented on those people who were of most support to them, *'mentor like senior colleagues', 'family encouragement and full support was a critical element in pursuing a career. My husband was 100 per cent behind me on all my career decisions. He totally believes in my ability'* and *'great sponsorship from a senior leader who had a voice in the business.'* (**Survey quotes**)

Having good networks is a great starting point and certainly many of the people in it will provide you with support, advice and feedback. However, on occasions you may feel that there are particular aspects of your behavior that you would like to understand more about and therefore would welcome receiving feedback from a trusted colleague or friend. In our experience it is often best to be specific rather than simply asking for feedback about, for instance, your presentation skills. Undoubtedly if you select an appropriate person to give you the feedback you will gain some insight into your performance and skills as a presenter. However, by adopting a more structured approach you can get even more valuable feedback to help you develop. So if you do want to improve your presentation skills you may like to follow this process. Firstly start by asking an appropriate trusted colleague to observe your behavior during the next presentation you give. Then indicate which aspects of the presentation you would like them to focus on – this could be the structure, the content, your delivery, how you cope with questions – whatever area you feel will be of most help. By framing the feedback you are more likely to get more specific comments that will be useful for your development.

As we have indicated, having a wide network is excellent but more important is the ability to leverage that network when appropriate. More than once in our research we heard about the power of the old boys' network (and not usually in a positive way, more as a way that excludes women). Wouldn't it be great if in future we could hear about the various women's networks or even just people networks that act as supporters for our success!!

MY CAREER STRATEGY – HOW

Think about how you want to present yourself when talking about your career aspirations. Be prepared for what you will say when anyone asks you, think through how you will present yourself and generally have a clear understanding of the impression you want to create. Clearly if you have not thought through your aspirations and what you want to achieve then you will be unable to present yourself in the best light. Most people when changing jobs or applying for a promotion will tailor their curriculum vitae to suit the role they are applying for and highlight relevant experience and qualifications and then think through examples of things they could talk about during an interview. But, interviews are not the only opportunity available to you for positioning yourself in relation to your career ambitions – you never know when you will take part in a casual conversation at work or in your social life where you will have the opportunity to talk about your career future. In Fiona's role as an executive coach and trainer she often asks her clients about their long term career aspirations. Few people are clear about their plans and ambition; some people only have a vague idea and find it difficult to articulate.

One way to help you to articulate your career aspirations is to think of yourself as a brand – just like any other product. The following model is one approach to this:

Brand me

Adapted from – Dent & Brent 2010:
The Leaders Guide To Influence

The work you have done so far should help you answer the questions in the brand model and enable you to have a clear picture of 'Brand Me'. The hard part is distilling this into coherent chunks so that you can present and promote yourself and your brand in a way that is memorable and meaningful to others and projects you in a positive and impressive way. On our training courses we often ask people to present an 'elevator pitch', the idea being they have someone's attention for only a few minutes and the challenge is to present their topic in such a way that it is influential and memorable. We would suggest that you develop a short and succinct 'elevator pitch' which you can use in any situation where someone asks you about your career aspirations or ambitions. Here are some tips which will help you to develop this:

■ Focus on your passions – your confidence and energy will then shine through.

- Remember it's about expressing what you are all about – state your brand clearly, concisely and confidently.
- Leave them wanting more – your aim is to influence people sufficiently that they want to enter a dialogue and engage with you in more detail.
- It's not about slogans or logos or slickness – be authentic and genuine, this will be much more effective.
- Think about your statement as your own personal advertisement for who you are, what you stand for and where you plan to go in your career.
- Listen to feedback that others give you and constantly refine your brand to keep it up to date.

Self promotion is important as no one has your interests at heart more than you do. Be prepared and take every appropriate opportunity to share your career aspirations with others and to create the impression of a switched on and focused professional who knows what you want to achieve.

MY CAREER STRATEGY – THE CAREER PLAN

The stages presented so far in this chapter provide you with ideas, tools and techniques to collect data, review, reflect and consolidate. Now that you have a clear idea of your career ambitions and aspirations we recommend that you create a career plan. We believe that by writing things down and then sharing what you have written with others you are more likely to achieve your goals. Of course it is important to recognize that plans are changeable, especially in today's business environment, so we would suggest that you develop your career plan a bit like a route map with milestones (personal goals) along the way and review this route map on a regular basis to ensure it continues to move in the right direction. If not adapt it. We would suggest 12-month, three-year and five-year milestones – you should decide on the timing of the milestones to suit you.

My career route map

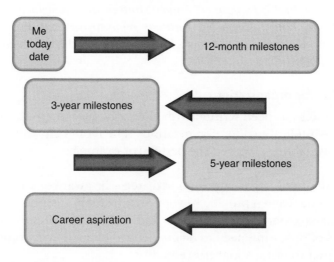

Thoughts for individuals

In order to ensure you are on the right track for a successful career you should:

- **Develop and understand your career aspirations** – be specific and develop a personal mission statement as a goal to aim for.
- **Know what you have got going for you** – use all the resources available to you to understand your strengths, weaknesses and development needs.
- **Identify and leverage those people who can support and help you** – recognize that you are not alone; other people can and will help you.
- **Prepare a personal pitch so that you can share your career ambitions clearly and succinctly with others** – be clear about what you want to achieve in your career and work out ways to share this with others
- **Have a plan** – by understanding your career landscape you can then develop your route map towards your career goals.

Finally, as one of the respondents to our questionnaire stated *'I can't help thinking that if I'd been a bit more strategic and thoughtful about my career I may have taken a less tortuous route to my goal, my advice to younger women would be to know what you want to achieve, develop a plan and go for it.'*

Thoughts for organizations

This chapter has been written with the individual in mind. However, there are implications for organizations. The more help and structure that is available for women the better. For example:

- **It's all about organizational attitude** – be aware of and celebrate the value women provide in your organization – attitudes in many business environments remain old fashioned. These outmoded ways of operating need to be challenged by men and women alike in order to bring about true equality.
- **Develop and understand women's career aspirations** – be sure that this help is formalized beyond the first few years when graduates join the organization – and be sure it doesn't simply rely on line mangers. *'I'm just back from maternity leave but my boss has said he won't bother with an appraisal as I haven't been here for the past year. Everyone else in my department had an appraisal. I pointed out that the appraisal discussion is also supposed to be forward looking but he still didn't see any need for a meeting.'* **(Survery quote)**
- **Find ways to create flexibility in your career planning and talent management structures** – lots of options are age-related, e.g., international experience in the early 30s which disadvantages women who have young families. Set up a working group to review how career planning can better match individual circumstances.
- **Target women at middle management level** – help them identify key skills (or experiences) that they need to gain, e.g., run regular development workshops. Find ways to identify people who will support and help them, e.g., sponsors, mentors and coaches.
- **Provide opportunities for coaching and mentoring** – many of the women in our research recognized the importance of their coach/mentor for their career success. Those who didn't have a coach/mentor commented that they thought this would have been beneficial.

10

FINAL THOUGHTS

In this short chapter we take a look at what the future might hold for women – fact or fiction? Time will tell. The first part is about what's happening now.

The weather was bad on this particular day and most planes were delayed for hours; some eventually were cancelled. In the business lounge at the airport many people sat glued to a Kindle or mobile phone but others drifted over to join small groups around the edge of the room. In one place a group of smartly dressed businesswomen talked about destinations, the weather and who knew the latest up-date on the airport situation; then the conversation turned towards the issues for women in business. One person said, *'I'm the most senior woman in my organisation and often when I go to chair meetings I'll be the only woman there ...'*

A younger woman in her 30s commented, *'I work for a great company with a fantastic policy on diversity but I notice that when I look beyond my level there are few women managers.'* Someone else added, *'I work for a French company – we're one of the best in our sector so that makes it a great place to work but it's full of alpha males so there's lots of macho behaviors and some sexist attitudes.'*

The view from another country highlights the stereotypes – *'the business I work in is definitely tougher on women – men get forgiven far more often and there are stereotypes about different areas. It's OK for women who want to be in HR, marketing or PR but not so easy if you want a career in engineering or operations.'* Another woman in her 30s observed that *'being a working woman is tough but it gets much tougher when you become a working mother as well.'*

Someone else had overheard the earlier comments and moved closer to the group saying,

> I work for a multinational and recently moved to a new job in Spain where a lot depends on who you know. It's called 'enchufado' – literally

'plugged in' which means well connected and this often includes guys rather than women managers. Earlier in my career I worked for a while in the UK public sector where there are similar groups – we called it the old boys' network. It's rather like attending one of the elite grandes écoles in France. Sometimes it's unintentional stuff like the senior team organised golf and sport events which created a closer group back at work; women are either not invited or don't want to attend and so are excluded from this 'insider' track.

But as the conversation continued others commented to say they have never been judged simply by gender. Their boss, their boss's boss or a chief executive had helped them; encouraged them and coached them giving them confidence that they could be great business leaders.

Roll forward to the year 2022 and imagine the same place, the same people but a different conversation which shows how things could change to create a better environment for women. *'The senior executive team in my organisation is now roughly 50/50 men and women. It's a great environment where everyone is judged only on ability not by gender.'*

Another spoke about their situation, *'I work for a German company – we're one of the best in our sector so that makes it a great place to work and it's a collegiate attitude where we all help one another to be more effective. Sexist comments used to be heard a few years ago but these days they would not be tolerated by any of our senior team'*. The woman colleague she was travelling with added – *'the business I work in treats women and men the same and there's lots of support for working parents. We did have stereotypes in the past about women working in marketing etc., but these days any career is open to them.'*

Another improvement highlighted is *'being a working woman and working mother has in the past been nearly impossible but now it's so simple with my company. We have a policy that anyone can work from home with occasional visits to the office – and we stick to it. The culture used to be solely office-based just a few years ago – presenteeism was everything if you wanted promotion here.'*

And the final thought is for the next generation of women leaders – *'before my daughter went to school I decided that I did not want her to ever have to think about discrimination in the way that my generation has had to do. Women now are treated equally.'*

APPENDIX A: A TIMELINE OF WOMEN'S ACHIEVEMENTS, 1903 TO 2011

The following list of dates and names highlights some of the achievements for women in business, politics and other areas of interest. It starts with some contemporary events and goes back to 1903. The list is illustrative rather than comprehensive and has been drawn from a number of sources including Wikipedia, women's biographical and speaker notes, books, articles, women's networks, our own knowledge and of course from company data. Some mark international or national achievements; other are company or sector milestones.

Dilma Rousseff is sworn in as Brazil's first woman President

2011

Dame Sally Davies is the first woman appointed Chief Medical Officer since the role was created in the 19th century. It is the most senior medical post in the UK

Yingluck Shinawatra is Thailand's first female prime minister

Madalina Suceveanu is appointed chief technology officer at France Telecom, the first woman to hold this appointment

Lieutenant Commander Sarah West takes command of HMS Portland and is the first woman in the Navy's 500-year history to command a British warship

St. Petersburg governor **Valentina Matvienko** is Russia's first woman to hold the third highest political appointment in the country as speaker of the Russian parliament

Maria Fekter is Austria's first female finance minister

Christine Lagarde, previously France's finance minister, is the first woman to head the International Monetary Fund since it was created in 1944. Earlier in 1999, at Baker & McKenzie, she became the first female chair of a global law firm

Jill Abramson is the first female executive editor at the *New York Times* since it was founded 160 years ago (the post is one of the most senior roles in American journalism)

Japan's largest brokerage house, Nomura, appointed its first female chief financial officer **Junko Nakagawa**. Press comments note that such an appointment is rare in Japan as most senior business appointments are held by men

Randy Lai is the first female managing director at McDonald's Singapore

Jill McDonald is the first female chief executive at McDonald's UK

Women for the first time take the majority of seats in the Swiss Cabinet

Yekaterina Mayering-Mikadze, a Georgian woman, is the first female ambassador to Saudi Arabia

Kholoud Adnan Mousa, a Deloitte auditor based in Jeddah, is the first woman to be awarded a Certified Public Accountant license in Saudi Arabia

Julia Gillard is the first female Prime Minister of Australia

Laura Cioli is awarded the 'Master of Masters' by Bocconi Business School in Italy. She is Chief Operating Officer at Sky Italia and the first woman to receive this title

Siza Mzimela is the first female CEO of South African Airways

Hannelore Kraft is elected president, and is the first woman to take this role, of the Bundesrat (which represents Germany's 16 states at the federal level)

Beth Mooney is the first female chief of a top 20 US bank at KeyCorp

2010 **Election of the largest number of women MPs in the UK** – 143. Between 1945 (when 24 women were elected) and 1992 (60 women were elected) the numbers remained low, the big change which caught the media's attention came in 1997 when 120 women were elected and photos of the new Prime Minister Tony Blair and the women MPs made headline news around the world

Sophie Hine, **Fiona O'Connor**, **Kate Malia**, **Natalie Watson** and Branch Manager **Glynis Gunning-Stevenson** are one of the first all-women management teams to run a John Lewis store (in Purley Way, Croydon, London)

Ari Fuji is Japan's first female captain pilot for commercial flights; she works for JAL Express Co

Angelika Dammann as chief human resources officer is appointed to the board of software maker SAP Gobal, which is the 2nd German blue chip company to appoint a woman at this level (the first is Siemens, 2008)

Abi Sekimitsu is the first woman appointed as editor in Reuters Japan

Ana Botín at Santander is the first woman chief of a major UK bank

Baroness Catherine Ashton is appointed EU Foreign Minister and is the first woman High Representative at the EU – she also was the first woman British commissioner and the first woman trade commissioner

Anne Jarvis is the first female librarian at Cambridge University, the first in its 650-year history

Chanda Kochhar is appointed CEO at ICICI Bank, the first woman leader of a private sector bank in India

Simone Bagel-Trah (Germany) at Henkel becomes the first female head of a DAX-listed company

2009

The first four women MPs are elected in Kuwait – **Aseel al-Awadhi, Rola Dashti, Salwa al-Jassar** and **Massuma al-Mubarak,** who also became the country's first female Cabinet Minister

Irina Georgieva Bokova is elected to become UNESCO's first female Director General

Elinor Ostrom, from Indiana University, USA, is the first woman to win a Nobel prize in Economics

Quentin Bryce is the first female (and 25th) Governor-General in Australia

Maria Bashir is appointed prosecutor general in Afghanistan, and she is the first woman to hold this senior role

Spain appoints a majority female cabinet for the first time. Jose Luis Rodriguez Zapatero selected 9 female ministers among the 17 appointments

Eva Habil is the first woman elected mayor in Egypt in Komboha – her father was also Mayor of that town

Ellen Kullman is appointed chief executive of DuPont, and it is the first time in DuPont's 206-year history that a woman has taken the most senior job

Khulood Ahmed Jawan Al Dhaheri is the first woman judge appointed in the United Arab Emirates

Anne Pringle is the first female British Ambassador to Russia

2008

Barbara Kux joins the Board of Directors at Siemens AG, and it is the first time in the company's over 160-year history that a woman has been appointed. She also becomes the first woman director of any German DAX 30 company

Norma Graham is Scotland's first female chief constable – appointed at Fife where she had been deputy chief constable since 2005

Ann Dunwoody is first female four-star general in the United States Army; her husband, father, grandfather and great-grandfather all had military careers

Ingela Bruner becomes the first female vice chancellor of an Austrian university, at the University of Natural Resources and Life Sciences in Vienna

Nancy Pelosi is the first female Speaker in the US Congress – in the House of Representatives

Drew Gilpin Faust is the first woman president at Harvard University

Hilary Clinton is the first woman Presidential candidate in the US

Fozia Jamelah is appointed managing director of RHB Islamic Bank in Malaysia and is the first woman to head an Islamic bank

2007

Pratibha Devisingh Patil is elected as the 12th President of India and the first woman to hold this job

Ghada Al Edreesy is the first Saudi woman to join DHL Saudi Arabia

Christine Lagarde (in France) is the first woman appointed as a finance minister in any G8 country (Global 8 countries are Germany, France, Italy, Japan, UK, Russia, Canada and US; (the European Union is also involved but does not host or chair meetings)

Angela Merkel, leader of the Christian Democratic Union, is Germany's first woman chancellor

Fran Allen, who spent her career at IBM, is the first woman to be awarded the prestigious A.M.Turing Award (the engineering equivalent of the Nobel prize)

Due to the merger of Lucent and Alcatel **Patricia Russo**, as CEO of Alcatel-Lucent (2006–2008), is the first woman to lead a company quoted on France's principal stock exchange, the CAC 40

Portia Lucretia Simpson-Miller is Jamaica's 7th Prime Minister and the first woman to hold this job

Letizia Moratti is elected as the first woman mayor of Milan, Italy

PepsiCo announce that **Indra Nooyi**, chief financial officer, will become Chairman and CEO; the 5th CEO and first female CEO in the company

2006

Rana Salhab is admitted to the partnership of Deloitte, and is the first woman partner at any professional services organization in the Middle East

Monika Harms is the first female attorney general in Germany

June Venters is the first woman solicitor in the UK to be appointed as Queen's Council

Ester Levanon is the first woman chief executive at the Tel Aviv Stock Exchange

Michelle Bachelet is Chile's first female president

At Anglo American, one of the world's largest mining companies, the FTSE 100's third woman chief executive is appointed. She is **Cynthia Carroll** and the first woman, and also the first non South-African, to run the company

Agnes Jongerius is the first **2005** **Debra Covey** is BT's first woman female president of Holland's managing director of wholesale largest trade union, Federal operations, one of the most Transportation, FNV senior jobs at the group

Bente Landsnes is the first woman to head the Oslo stock exchange

Fru Hazlitt, managing director, Yahoo UK wins the First Woman of Media Award

Nahed Taher is the first woman to head a Middle Eastern bank; she is co-founder and chief executive at Gulf One Investment Bank

Lubna Olayan is elected to the **2004** **Güler Sabanci** takes over as board of Saudi Hollandi Bank, chairman at Sabanci Holdings – and is the first woman in Saudi she is the first woman to head a to become a director of a publicly major Turkish corporation listed company

Clover Moore is the 82nd Lord Mayor of Sydney and the first woman to hold the job

Susan Hockfield, Provost of Yale, is the first woman (and 16th) president at MIT, the Massachusetts Institute of Technology

Judy Boynton, Finance Director, **2003** **Sharon Allen**, a Los Angeles is promoted to join the Executive partner, is the first woman to Board at Royal Dutch Shell chair Deloitte's board; this also is Group, the first woman to reach a first for the big four accounting that level in the company firms

Sally Buckles is the Great Lakes regional managing partner. She is the second woman to head one of Deloitte & Touche's nine regions in the US

Brenda Hale is the first woman to become a law lord (and sit in the highest court in the UK)

Dora Bakoyannis is the first **2002** **Laura D'Andrea Tyson** is London woman elected as mayor of Business School's first female Athens, Greece Dean

Members of the Athenaeum Club, London vote to admit women members

Gail Kelly is the first woman CEO of a major Australian bank or top 15 companies – she was appointed as CEO at Westpac in 2008

Clara Furse is the first **2001** **Baroness Sarah Hogg** is the female chief executive of the first woman to head a FTSE100 200-year-old London Stock company at 3i Exchange

Fran Mainella is the first woman (and 16th Director) of the US National Park Service

Harriet Harman is the first woman to be appointed as Solicitor General

Ann Goddard is for many years the Old Bailey's only permanent woman judge

Janet Gaymer is the first woman senior partner at Simmons & Simmons, and the first at any Top 10 City law firm

Barbara Sparer-Fuchs is the first female head of an Austrian county court

Christine Bortenländer is **2000** appointed as the first female Managing Director of the Munich Stock Exchange

Merlyn Lowther is appointed **1999** Chief Cashier at the Bank of England (1999–2003) and the first woman to hold this job

Ann McBrien is appointed Vice President of Sales in Procter & Gamble, the first woman to hold that role

Patricia Woertz is Chevron Products Co. president, the first woman in that senior role at Chevron and the first in the oil industry

Clara Freeman is the first woman appointed to the executive board in the history of Marks & Spencer

Susan Arnold takes global responsibility for Procter & Gamble's personal beauty business and becomes the first woman to reach president level in the company

Carly Fiorina is president and chief executive at Hewlett Packard and the first woman chosen to lead a Fortune 50 company

Caroline Aigle is the first French woman to graduate as a fighter pilot in the French Air Force

Ruth Anderson is the first **1998** woman to join the KPMG board

Marjorie Scardino becomes the **1997** first woman to head a FTSE 100 company in the UK when she takes the top job at the media company Pearson

Elisabeth Bleyleben-Koren becomes the first female head of a larger bank, Erste Bank, in Austria

Madeleine Albright's appointment as the 64th Secretary of State was unanimously approved by the Senate on January 23, 1997 and she is the first female Secretary of State

For the first time in 1997 women are permitted to join the Vienna Philharmonic Orchestra as full members, **Anna Lelkes** is the first woman to join and in 2010 **Albena Danailova**, a Bulgarian, is the first appointed as concertmaster

Jacquelyn Zehner is the first **1996**
woman bond trader to be made a
partner at Goldman Sachs

Nora Wu is the first female **1995** **Pauline Clare** is appointed Chief
manager in Arthur Andersen Constable at Lancashire, one of
Shanghai offices the largest provincial forces in
the UK. She is the first woman
to hold this job and joined the
police when she was 17

Marie-Claude Peyrache, Senior **1994**
Vice President Communications,
is the first woman to join France
Telecom's Executive Committee

1993 **Janet Reno** is the first woman to
hold office of Attorney General of
the US

Naina Lal Kidwai is the first **1992** **Betty Bothroyd**, a Labour MP, is
Indian woman to graduate from elected Speaker of the House of
Harvard Business School; she is Commons (1992–2000), and is
Country Head of HSBC in India the first woman elected to hold
this office
Carol Bartz (at Autodesk) is the
first female chief executive of **Ann-Marit Sæbønes** is the first
a major software company. She woman elected mayor of Oslo,
later joined Yahoo in 2009 Norway

Barbara Mills is the first female
director of Public Prosecutions

Edith Cresson is France's first **1991** **Julie Ann Gibson** is the RAF's
female prime minister first female pilot

Mary Robinson is the first **1990** **Judy Lewent** assumes the
female President of Ireland. She position of chief financial officer
asked women to vote for her to at Merck and is the first woman
help ensure she won the election to serve as the CFO of a major
corporation in the US
Margaret Salmon is the first
woman to be appointed to **Catherine Tizard** is the first
the BBC Television Board of female Governor-General in New
Management Zealand – she also was the first
female mayor of Auckland in 1983

Christiane Scrivener and **Vasso Papandreou** are the first female Commissioners appointed at the European Union (the EU was founded in 1958 following the Treaty of Rome)

1989 **Margaret Turner-Warwick** is the first woman President of the Royal College of Physicians (1989–1992)

Ellen R. Schneider-Lenné is the first woman to be appointed as an executive director at Deutsche Bank (or at any other major German bank)

1988 **Katherine Hudson** is appointed head of IT and becomes the first woman corporate vice president in Kodak

Benazir Bhutto, Prime Minister of Pakistan from 1993–1996 is the first woman leader of a Muslim state

Lynn Barton is British Airways' first female pilot. Also in 2008 she made history by piloting the first flight into Heathrow's Terminal 5 when it opened

1987 **Census Bureau** reports that the average woman in the US earns 68 cents for every dollar earned by a man

Corazon Aquino, President of the Philippines from 1986–1992, is the first woman to hold that post and Asia's first female president

1986

Brenda Dean is elected General Secretary of SOGAT (Society of Graphical and Allied Trades), the first woman to head a major trade union in the UK

1984 **Beverly Lynn Burns** became the first woman to captain a Boeing 747 jumbo jet

Milka Planinc is appointed Prime Minister in Yugoslavia and is the first woman leader of a Communist country

1982 **Anne Krueger** is appointed Vice President, Economics and Research and becomes the World Bank's first female Vice President

Pirjo Hggman and **Flor Isava Fonseca** (from Finland and Venezuela respectively) are the first women members elected to the International Olympics Committee

1981 **Dr. Gro Harlem Brundtland** is Norway's first female Prime Minister (and also the youngest person appointed to the role)

Sandra Day O'Connor is the first woman seated on the US Supreme Court. She was nominated by Ronald Reagan to fulfill his campaign promise to break the gender barrier at the Supreme Court

1980 **Vigdís Finnbogadóttir** is the first woman President of Iceland (1980–1996) and the first woman President in Europe

Margaret Thatcher is the first female Prime Minister in the UK

1979 **Elizabeth Butler-Sloss** is the first woman High Court judge in England and Wales

Rosemary Murray joins the board at Midland Bank. She is not only the first female director at Midland but also the first female director of any of the major UK clearing banks

1978

1977 **Hanna Gray** is the first woman to serve as University President (acting) at Yale University

Women are permitted to join the officer training programme for the Royal Navy

1976 **Anne Warburton** is Britain's first female ambassador (in Denmark)

Anne Armstrong is America's first woman ambassador to the UK

1975 **Rosemary Murray**, President of New Hall, is the first woman Vice-Chancellor at Cambridge

Christine Davy is the first woman in Australia to pilot a passenger airline for Connair

1974 **Sally Murphy** is the first woman to fly helicopters in the United States Army

Jeanne M. Holm is the first woman appointed as a two-star General in the US Air Force

1973 On 26th March **Muriel Wood** and **Susan Shaw** are among the first few (10) women admitted as members of the London Stock Exchange after years of campaigning by women working in the financial service sector

Juantia Kreps is the first woman director at the New York Stock Exchange

1972 **Katharine Graham** of the *Washington Post* is the first female executive to run a Fortune 500 company (the *Washington Post* joined the list in 1972)

At Banco Pastor **Carmela Arias y Diaz de Rábago** is appointed as executive president of the bank, the first woman in Spain to hold this appointment

1971

1970 **Kamaljit Sandhu** is the first woman judge appointed in India

Golda Meir is elected the first woman Prime Minister in Israel

1969

Gabrielle Defrenne challenged Sabena, the Belgium airline, on the grounds of discrimination as female cabin crew were required to retire at 40, whereas men could continue working

1968 **Barbara H. Liskov** is the first woman in the US to be awarded a PhD in computer science from Stanford University

Shirley Chisholm is the first black woman to join Congress in the US

Hélène Ploix is one of the first female MBA delegates at INSEAD business school in France

Muriel Siebert is the first woman to take a seat on the New York Stock Exchange (of around 1,300 members). In 2007 in honor of her 40 years as a member and for being the first woman to join she is invited to ring the closing bell for the day's trading. Her autobiography 'Changing the Rules – Adventures of a Wall Street Maverick' is published in 2002 by Simon and Schuster

1967

Indira Gandhi, Prime Minister of India from 1966–1977 is the first woman to hold that post

1966 IBM's first female systems engineer in Austria – **Beate Hager** – becomes the first female instructor at IBM's Training Centre in Vienna

Civil Rights Act outlaws sex discrimination in the US

1964

Betty Nicholls is Manager of Portsmouth North End branch of National Westminster Bank and becomes one of the first female bank managers in the UK

Equal Pay Act passed by the US Congress

1963

Russian cosmonaut **Valentina Tereshkova** is the first woman in space; thousands of women in Moscow were so delighted on hearing the news that they gathered in Red Square to celebrate her achievement and she became a national hero. Later she also is the first woman appointed as a general officer in the Russian armed forces

Following a vote among faculty members, **women** are fully admitted to join the Harvard Business school Master of Business Administration programme – some had previously qualified in associated colleges. Known as the 'first eight' to have joined the MBA programme (which first ran in 1910), the women, who all graduated in 1965, were Elaine Luthy, Elizabeth Trotman, Cecilia Rauch, Caryl Maclaughlin Brackenridge, Susan Lauer Holt, Lynne Sherwood, Michelle Roos Turnovsky and Dixie Marchant

Roma Mitchell is the first woman QC in Australia

1962

1961

Elisabeth Schwarzhaupt is the first woman to head a federal ministry in Germany (Minister of Health)

Sirimavo Bandaranaike is the first woman elected as Prime Minister in Sri Lanka (re-elected in 1970 and in 1994) and the world's first female Head of Government. She initially stood for election following her husband's assassination

1960

Mary Roebling is the first female governor of the American Stock Exchange

1958

Hilda Harding is the first woman bank manager at Barclays, Hanover Street, London, also a first for the UK banking industry

Lila Jones becomes the first woman manager at H.J. Heinz in Pittsburg, US

1956 **Dame Rose Helibron** is the first woman judge in England and Wales

Müfide İlhan is elected as the first woman mayor in Turkey and of Mersin **1950**

1949 **Eugenie Anderson** is the first woman appointed as a United States Ambassador – to Denmark

Bessie Leister Dempsey is Boeing's first female engineer **1948**

1947 **Ida Townsend**, export manager, joined the board of Glaxo, the company's first woman director

Italian women vote for the first time **1946**

1945 **1941–45** Millions of women in the UK and in US enter work force during the Second World War – 'Rosie the Riveter' was the name of the woman featured in a poster campaign across America to encourage women to take up factory roles

Ruth Leach Amonette is IBM's first woman vice president **1943**

1942 **Mary Malcolm** is one of the first two female announcers at BBC Television

Homai Vyarawalla is India's first woman photojournalist and this is still true when she retired in 1970. In 2010 she is awarded the Padma Vibhushan, one of India's highest civilian honors **1941**

1937 **Clare Reckert** is the first female financial/business reporter at the *New York Times*

Lettie Pate Whitehead Evans `1934`
at Coca-Cola is the first woman
to become a director of a major
American business

`1933` **Frances Perkins** is sworn in as
Secretary of Labor, first woman in
the US cabinet

Lilian Wyles is the first `1932`
woman Chief Inspector in the
Police. She joined London's
Metropolitan police force in 1919
and the Criminal Investigation
Department (CID) in 1922. A
book about her career, A Woman
at Scotland Yard–Reflections on
the Struggles and Achievements
of Thirty Years in the
Metropolitan Police, is published
by Faber and Faber in 1952

`1930` **Ellen Church**, a registered nurse,
convinced Boeing managers that
women could work as stewards;
she became the first female cabin
crew – joining a flight for San
Francisco and women nurses
joined on the Model 80A planes

Margaret Bondfield is appointed `1929`
Minister of Labour and becomes
the first woman to join the
British Cabinet

`1928` For the first time **women** in
the UK can vote on the same
terms as men (all those over 21
could now vote)

Nellie Tayloe Ross inaugurated `1925`
in Wyoming, first woman
governor in US. In the same year
Miriam Amanda Ferguson is
elected in Texas

Carrie Morrison is the first **1923** woman to become a solicitor; she was one of four women who passed the Law Society's examinations in 1922 – the others were **Maud Crofts, Mary Sykes** and **Mary Pickup**

Agnes Macphail is the first **1921** female to take her seat in the Canadian House of Commons

Ivy Williams is the first female barrister in the UK

Women are called for jury service for the first time in the UK Central Criminal Court

Women became eligible for **1920** admission as full members of Oxford University and could take a degree. At Cambridge University women were given the title of a degree a year later, in 1921, but not allowed to participate in University government. Only after an honorary degree is given to the Queen Mother in 1948 are women awarded degrees. And it is not until 1956 women are permitted to take their examinations in the same room as the men

Jantina Tammes is the first **1919** woman in Holland to be appointed as a University professor – at the University of Groningen

Nancy Astor is the first woman MP in the UK to take her seat in the House of Commons

National Woman's Party begins **1917** picketing the White House in the US for suffrage on July 14 – women are given the right to vote in 1920

1916 **Jeannette Rankin** elected to the US Congress, the first woman to join Congress

Edith Smith was the first `1915`
policewoman in Britain
appointed (in Grantham) to have
full powers of arrest

`1911` **First International Women's
Day**

Josephine Gordon Stuart `1909`
and **Eveline MacLaren** are
the first women to graduate as
Bachelors of Law from Edinburgh
University, Scotland

`1908` **Elizabeth Garrett Anderson** is
elected at Aldeborough, the first
woman mayor in England. She
was also the first woman to gain
a medical degree in England in
1865 by taking the examinations
with the Society of Apothecaries,
which did not specifically
forbid women from taking their
examinations – the medical
schools banned her and other
women

`1903`

Women's Trade Union League
founded in the US to support
working women

Note: Every effort has been made to ensure the data are accurate and
we would welcome any corrections or additional examples.

APPENDIX B:
QUESTIONNAIRE QUANTITATIVE ANALYSIS

Survey: Women Leaders' Questionnaire
Responses received: 1406

1. What is your age group (years)?

Response	Count	Percentage
30 and under	57	4.1
31–40	405	28.9
41–50	641	45.8
51–60	278	19.8
61+	20	1.4

2. Nationality:

Response	Count	Percentage
UK	1020	72.9
Rest of Europe	257	18.4
International	123	8.8

3. Organizational level:

Response	Count	Percentage
Junior manager	80	5.8
Middle manager	342	24.8
Senior manager	544	39.4
Director/Chief Executive	413	29.9

4. How many people are employed in total in your organization (approximately)?

Response	Count	Percentage
Under 100	179	12.8
101–500	242	17.3
501–1000	149	10.7
1000+	827	59.2

5. Please indicate your earnings level – salary and bonus.

Response	Count	Percentage
Less than £20k	18	1.3
£21k–£40k	158	11.5
£41k–£60k	364	26.4
£61k–£80k	251	18.2
£81k–£100k	215	15.6
£101k–£150k	240	17.4
£151k+	133	9.6

6. During your career please indicate the people who have supported you in achieving your goals. Please tick all that apply.

Response	Count	Percentage
Boss	1220	86.8
Colleagues	1084	77.1
Internal Coach (a relationship based on developing your skills)	159	11.3
External Coach	462	32.9
Internal mentor (a relationship with a more experienced role model)	413	29.4
External mentor	277	19.7
Family	976	69.4
Friends	772	54.9
Other (please specify)	106	7.5

7. How would you describe your primary leadership style? Tick one box only.

Response	Count	Percentage
Participative – you actively involve others in discussion and decision making	396	28.3
Situational – you vary your style to suit the situation	377	26.9
Visionary – you inspire others through your energy and commitment	233	16.6
Transactional – you give directions and expect them to be met	13	0.9
Value based – you lead based on strong personal values	130	9.3
Intuitive – a more instinctive approach where both people and the situation are considered; gut-feel.	217	15.5
Hierarchical – driven by level and status	1	0.1
Other (please specify)	34	2.4

8. Do you feel your primary leadership style is driven by your organization's prevailing leadership approach?

Response	Count	Percentage
Yes	389	27.9
No	1007	72.1

9. On a scale of 1 to 10 shown below, how much do you agree men and women are judged differently in your organization with regard to leadership style and behavior?

Response	Count	Percentage
1 Strongly disagree	106	7.6
2	98	7.0
3	132	9.5
4	99	7.1
5	128	9.2
6	151	10.8
7	203	14.6
8	273	19.6
9	109	7.8
10 Strongly agree	95	6.8

10. On a scale of 1 to 10 shown below, in your opinion is it harder for women to succeed in your organization compared to your male colleagues?

Response	Count	Percentage
1 Strongly disagree	152	10.9
2	117	8.4
3	129	9.2
4	98	7.0
5	116	8.3
6	120	8.6
7	223	16.0
8	219	15.7
9	107	7.7
10 Strongly agree	116	8.3

11. On a scale of 1 to 10 shown below, are men and women judged equally with regard to promotion in your organization?

Response	Count	Percentage
1 Strongly disagree	54	3.9
2	43	3.1
3	79	5.7
4	105	7.6
5	167	12.0
6	158	11.4
7	179	12.9
8	205	14.8
9	174	12.6
10 Strongly agree	222	16.0

12. On the scale shown below, how important is work/life balance to you?

Response	Count	Percentage
1 Very unimportant	33	2.4
2	15	1.1
3	34	2.4
4	41	2.9
5	69	4.9
6	79	5.7
7	155	11.1
8	295	21.1
9	222	15.9
10 Very important	455	32.5

13. On the scale shown below, looking at your life today, how would you describe your work/life balance?

Response	Count	Percentage
1 Very poor	35	2.5
2	40	2.9
3	118	8.4
4	190	13.6
5	148	10.6
6	177	12.7
7	279	20.0
8	242	17.3
9	91	6.5
10 Excellent	78	5.6

14. If you have completed the Myers Briggs Type Indicator please indicate your best fit 4 letter type below:

Response	Count	Percentage
ISTJ	45	5.2
ISFJ	17	2.0
INFJ	26	3.0
INTJ	88	10.2
ISTP	16	1.9
ISFP	6	0.7
INFP	24	2.8
INTP	37	4.3
ESTP	22	2.5
ESFP	19	2.2
ENFP	85	9.8
ENTP	121	14.0
ESTJ	88	10.2
ESFJ	46	5.3
ENFJ	72	8.3
ENTJ	152	17.6

NOTES AND REFERENCES

CHAPTER 2

1 Published by Elsevier, 2004.
2 'Winning the talent war for women: Sometimes it takes a revolution' by Douglas McCracken, *Harvard Business Review*, November/December 2000, Vol. 78, Issue 6, pp. 159–167.
3 KPMG fails to fairly promote women, Terry Baynes, published 2 June 2011 on Thomson Reuters Legal News, http://newsandinsight.thomsonreuters.com/Legal/News/2011/06_-_June/KPMG_fails_to_fairly_promote_women,_lawsuit_says/ accessed January 2012.
4 Female City bankers sue over sexism claims at Japanese bank Nomura, Richard Edwards, *Daily Telegraph*, 3 November 2009 http://www.telegraph.co.uk/finance/newsbysector/banksandfinance/6493677/Female-City-bankers-sue-over-sexism-claims-at-Japanese-bank-Nomura.html accessed January 2012.
5 'Tribunal refuses to review decision on Switalski £19m sex discrimination claim' by Guy Logan, *Personnel Today*, 15 August 2008.
6 'Morgan Stanley settles sex discrimination case for $54million' reported on The Ethical Corporation website, www.ethicalcorp.com/content.asp?ContentID=2383, accessed January 2011.
7 'Wal-Mart women denied discrimination class action', reported by the BBC, 20 June 2011. www.bbc.co.uk/news/world-us-canada-13845970, accessed June 2011.
8 *Public Servant, Private Woman* by Alix Meynell. Gollancz, 1988.
9 'Breaching the divide' by Jo Adetunji, the Guardian online article 17 August 2010, www.guardianpublic.co.uk/senior-management-women-local-authorities, accessed November 2010.
10 *Growth Company: Dow Chemical's First Century* by E. N. Brandt. Michigan State University Press, 1997, p. 344.
11 Holton, V, Rabbetts, J. (1997) *Women on the Board of Britains Top 200 Companies*, Ashridge Report.
12 *Beyond Race and Gender* by Roosevelt Thomas, Jr. American Management Association, 1991.
13 'Berlin may get a female Chancellor, but it's still a man's world' by Jody K. Biehl, 9 July 2005, Spiegel online, accessed August 2010. www.spiegel.de/international/0,1518,druck-371204,00.html
14 Watching China wiz, 19 August 2010. http://mobile.economist.com/business_16847828.php, accessed October 2010.
15 'Bank of Japan's first female chief says women being held back' by Adam Le and Masatsugu Horie, 17 August 2010, *Bloomberg Businessweek*. www.businessweek.

com/news/2010-08-17/boj-s-first-female-chief-says-women-being-held-back.html, accessed October 2010.

16 *Management Today*'s '"35 women under 35" 2010: Creating the future' by Emma de Vita and Hannah Prevett, *Management Today*, 1 July 2010.

17 *Women of the Street: Making It on Wall Street – The World's Toughest Business* by Sue Herera. John Wiley, 1997.

18 '20 Questions: Dominique Senequier' by Emma Jacobs, *Financial Times*, 6 August 2010.

19 '20 Questions: "Bling is a waste of time"' by Emma Jacobs, *Financial Times*, 8 October 2010.

20 'Some female CEOs shatter the pay ceiling' by Alexis Leondis, *International Herald Tribune*, 19 May 2010.

21 Reported in the Fortune 500 survey, http://money.cnn.com/magazines/fortune/fortune500/2011/womenceos/, accessed July 2011.

22 Davos 2009: Where are the women? By Morice Mendoza 26 January 2009, *Bloomberg Businessweek*. www.businessweek.com/globalbiz/content/jan2009/gb20090126_612317.htm, accessed 20 July 2010.

23 'Davos imposes gender quota' by Elena Moya, *Guardian*, 12 January 2011 www.guardian.co.uk/business/2011/jan/12/davos-imposes-gender-quota? INTCMP=SRCH

24 As reported by Gill Pimmer in 'Pay parity still a century away', *Financial Times*, 31 August 2011.

25 'Italy, with few women managers, lags developed country average' by Elisa Martinuzzi and Flavia Krause-Jackson, 30 June 2010, *Bloomberg Businessweek*. www.businessweek.com/news/2010-06-30/italy-with-few-women-managers-lags-developed-country-average.html, accessed 30 August 2010.

26 'Off-ramps and on-ramps: women's nonlinear career paths' by Sylvia Ann Hewlett, in *Women and Leadership*, edited by Barbara Kellerman and Deborah Rhode. Wiley, 2007.

27 'Flexibility key for women' by Widget Finn, *Guardian*, 20 July 2010 and German Women: Stuck at Home by Katrin Bennhold, *International Herald Tribune*, 29 June 2011.

28 'Jay is for juggling: Interview with Jay Hunt' by Maggie Brown, *Guardian*, 15 March 2010.

29 'Women matter 2010: Women at the top of corporations – making it happen' by McKinsey, 2010.

30 www.workingmother.com/BestCompanies/node/7818/list/4767, accessed September 2011.

31 'Working (part time) in the 21st century: In Netherlands, a practice that started with women is now spreading to men' by Katrin Bennhold, *International Herald Tribune*, 30 December 2010.

32 'Deutsche Telekom leads the way: blue-chip German companies oppose gender quotas' by Sven Böll and Michael Kröger, 16 March 2010, Der Spiegel online www. spiegel.de/international/germany/0,1518,683869,00.html

33 http://knowledge.insead.edu/Top-200-global-CEOs.cfm, accessed August 2011.

34 'European Board Diversity 2010: Is it getting easier to find women on European Boards?' by Laurence Monnery and Katrin Sier, Egon Zehnder www.egonzehnder.com/global/thoughtleadership/publications/articleindex/publication/id/17500237, accessed October 2010.

35 Data from the Brazilian Corporate Governance Institute quoted in Gender gap narrows in Brazil by Joe Leahy in *Financial Times*, 16 February 2011.

36 Lückerath-Rovers, Mijntje, The Dutch Female Board Index 2010 (September 9, 2010). Erasmus Institute Monitoring and Compliance, September 2010. Available at SSRN: http://ssrn.com/abstract=1722683, accessed January 2011.

37 '2010 UK Board Index: Current board trends and practices at major UK companies' by Spencer Stuart, see http://content.spencerstuart.com/sswebsite/pdf/lib/UKBI_2010_web.pdf, accessed January 2011.

38 'New Zealand Census of women's participation 2010' by New Zealand Human Rights Commission.

39 Quoted in profile of Gale Kelly, Westpac in 'Women at the top: The top 50 women in world business', edited by Michael Skapinker, Financial Times, 17 November 2010.

40 'Will women ever win the board game?' by James Quinn, Sunday Telegraph, 26 December 2010.

41 'Goal at Deutsche Telekom: More women as managers' by Nicola Clark, New York Times, 15 March 2010. www.nytimes.com/2010/03/16/business/global/16quota.html, accessed October 2010.

42 Blue-chip is a business phrase describing the most highly valued organizations on a stock exchange; it is borrowed from poker where blue chips (rather than red or white) are the most valuable.

43 'Superwoman's unequal battle: Top fund manager Helena Morrissey oversees £47bn of investment – as well as a family of nine children' by Tom Bawden, Guardian, 21 January 2011.

44 Reported in Nikk Magasin, March 2010, 'Companies want to recruit more women to top posts' www.nikk.no/?module=Articles;action=Article.publicShow;ID=1161, accessed January 2011. Data from the Global MBA Rankings sourced from http://www.ft.com/businesseducation/executiveeducation2011

45 Described in chapter 1, 'A woman's place is in the Boardroom: the roadmap' by Peninah Thomson, Jacey Graham and Tom Lloyd. Palgrave Macmillan, 2008.

46 One of the projects undertaken by Ursula Burns before she became CEO at Rank Xerox. 'How I did it... Xerox's former CEO on why succession shouldn't be a horse race' by Anne Mulcahy. Harvard Business Review, October 2010.

47 rankings.ft.com/businessschoolrankings/global-mba-rankings

48 Quoted in 'Will women be the major growth area for business schools?' By Liz Lightfoot, Independent, 8 April 2010.

49 Data published on Harvard website, www.hbs.edu/about/statistics/mba.html, accessed October 2010. 2011 data published on http://rankings.ft.com/exportranking/global-mba-rankings-2011/pdf, accessed January 2011 show that 36 percent of students are women.

50 Claire Pike Remembers, published on INSEAD's website, http://knowledge.insead.edu/claire-pike-on-INSEAD-101213.cfm?vid=507, accessed January 2011.

51 Women CEOs, Fortune, 26 July 2010, published online at CNN.money.com http://money.cnn.com/magazines/fortune/global500/2010/womenceos/, accessed October 2010.

52 In the mid 1960s Gordon Moore, Chairman of Intel, predicted that the number of transistors on a chip would rapidly double about every two years. This was precisely what did happen across the computing industry and so later this became known as 'Moore's Law'.

53 '25 years of retailing; 25 years of change? Reflecting on the position of women managers' by Adelina Broadbridge, Gender in Management, 2010, Vol. 25, No. 8.

54 'Where are the women in leadership in Australia?' by Leonie Still, Women in Management Review, 2006, Vol. 21, Issue 3.

55 'Where did all the British bosses of FTSE companies go?' By Louisa Peacock, *Daily Telegraph*, 3 February 2011.

56 Diversity on the *Forbes* Women Power List by Jenna Goudreau, published on Forbes Blogs, http://blogs.forbes.com/jennagoudreau/2010/10/06/diversity-on-the-forbes-power-women-list-michelle-obama-oprah-winfrey, accessed October 2010.

57 *First Among Equals: the Rise of IBM's First Female Corporate Vice President* by Ruth Amonette. Creative Arts, 2000.

58 'Expectations and achievement: empowering women from within' by and published by Accenture, March 2007. www.accenture.com/NR/rdonlyres/3E7A6651-7C19–44AD-A788-C68A99C10A67/0/2007IWDResearchReport_FINAL.pdf, accessed 4 August 2010.

59 'Male executives call for more women at the top' by Katrin Bennhold, *International Herald Tribune* 18 October 2010.

CHAPTER 3

1 'Breaking the glass ceiling begins at home' by Lucy Kellaway, *Financial Times* 22 November 2010.

2 The CIPD Learning and Talent Development Survey 2010 published by the CIPD, UK.

CHAPTER 4

1 'Sam Smith: I eventually learnt to be myself', *Sunday Times*, 20 September 2011.

2 Jack Grimston, 'Nah, forget it: lack of drive keeps women out of jobs'. *Sunday Times*, 20 September 2011.

CHAPTER 5

1 'Women on Boards' by Lord Davies. February 2011. Department of Business Innovation and Skills.

CHAPTER 6

1 'Our lessons in power: What can we learn from some of the 20th century's most noted leaders' by Brian Michael Till, *Independent*, 3 June 2011.

CHAPTER 7

1 The situation in the EU http://ec.europa.eu/social/main.jsp?catId=685&langId=en accessed March 2011.

2 Comments made at the Women as Leaders Institute of Directors conference, 23 November 2010.

3 'Past perspectives, future change: a study into the experiences of senior women in financial services' by Anne Murphy, 2011, published by Odgers Berndtson www.odgersberndtson.co.uk/gb/knowledge-insight/article/past-perspectives-future-change-executive-summary-3428/ accessed March 2011.

4 'Baroness of the boardrooms' by Heather Connon, *Observer*, 30 November 2003.
5 'Women told to speak their minds to get on in boardrooms' by Daniel Boffey, *Observer*, 19 June 2011.
6 Women's Leadership Development Survey published by Mercer, March 2011. See www.mercer.com/press-release/1409145 accessed May 2011.
7 Marjorie Scardino is chief executive of Pearson which owns the Financial Times newspaper and book publishers Penguin. Source: 'Pearson chief Marjorie Scardino questions fixation with female board' by Amanda Andrews, 28 February 2011 see http://uk.finance.yahoo.com/news/Pearson-chief-Marjorie-tele-347066211.html?x=0&.v=1 accessed June 2011.

CHAPTER 8

1 Elizabeth Garrett Anderson was an inspiring role model from much earlier times – she was the first woman to gain a medical qualification in England and later when she retired to East Anglia became the first woman mayor in 1908.
2 Madeleine Albright's appointment as the 64th Secretary of State was unanimously approved by the US Senate on January 23, 1997 – she became the first female Secretary of State.
3 '20 Questions: Amy Nelson-Bennett' by Emma Jacobs published in the *Financial Times* 20 January, 2011 http://cachef.ft.com/cms/s/0/8e2a04be-24e2-11e0-895d-00144feab49a.html#axzz1OUWwvB2w accessed July 2011.
4 Read the details in Leadership by Rudolph Guliani – the book shares a good deal of leadership wisdom as well as his vivid account of the 9/11 attack on New York. Published in 2002 by Little Brown.
5 Comments reported at the London Business Forum, October 2010.

FURTHER READING

'Women and Leadership: The State of Play and Strategies for Change' by Barbara Kellerman and Deborah L Rhode, Jossey Bass 2007.

'Living Leadership. A Practical Guide for Ordinary Heroes' by Binney, G; Wilke, G; & Williams, C., FT Prentice Hall 2005.

'The Leader's Guide to Influence: How to Use Soft Skills to Get Hard Results' by Dent, F. E. 2010 & Brent, M. by Pearson 2010.

'The Diversity Scorecard: Evaluating the Impact of Diversity on Organizational Performance' by Edward E. Hubbard, Elsevier 2004.

'Relax It's only Uncertainty' by Hodgson, P and White, R., FT Prentice Hall, 2001.

'Ambition and Gender at Work' by The Institute of Leadership and Management. 2011.

'Women on Boards' by Lord Davies. February 2011, Department of Business Innovation and Skills.

'The Female FTSE Board Report 2009' by Dr Ruth Sealy, Prof Susan Vinnicombe and Elena Doldor, Cranfield University, School of Management.

'Women Who Changed the World', Smith Davis Publishing 2006.

INDEX